THE THIRD LENS

To my guiding lights
Susanna and Anton

The Third Lens

Multi-ontology Sense-making and Strategic Decision-making

MIKA AALTONEN
Helsinki University of Technology, Finland

ASHGATE

Published by
Ashgate Publishing Limited
Gower House
Croft Road
Aldershot
Hampshire GU11 3HR
England

Ashgate Publishing Company
Suite 420
101 Cherry Street
Burlington, VT 05401-4405
USA

Ashgate website: http://www.ashgate.com

British Library Cataloguing in Publication Data
The third lens : multi-ontology sense-making and strategic decision-making
1. Decision making 2. Business planning
I. Aaltonen, Mika
658.4'03

Library of Congress Cataloging-in-Publication Data
The third lens : multi-ontology sense-making and strategic decision-making / edited by Mika Aaltonen.
p. cm.
Includes bibliographical references and index.
ISBN 978-0-7546-4798-0
1. Decision-making. 2. Management. 3. Ontology. I. Aaltonen, Mika.

HD30.23.T453 2007
658.4'012--dc22

2007001512

ISBN 978-0-7546-4798-0

Printed and bound in Great Britain by Antony Rowe Ltd, Chippenham, Wiltshire.

Contents

Part 4: Conclusions

List of Figures and Tables

Annex in Chapter 5

List of Abbreviations

CAS	Complex Adaptive System
CES	Complex Evolving Systems
CEWARN	Conflict Early Warning and Response Mechanism
CMI	Conflict Management Initiative
DBR	Deutsche Bank Research
E:CO	Emergence: Complexity and Organizations
ECOWAS	Economic Community of West African States
EIS	Executive Information Systems
FAO	Food and Agricultural Organization
FDI	Foreign Direct Investment
GDP	Gross Domestic Product
IGAD	Inter-Governmental Authority on Development
IMF	International Monetary Fund
LSE	London School of Economics
NAM	Non-Aligned Countries
NATO	North Atlantic Treaty Organization
NGO	Non-Governmental Organization
OECD	Organization for Economic Co-operation and Development
ORCI	Office for Research and the Collection of Information
PISA	Programme for International Student Assessment
PPP	Purchasing Power Parity
R&D	Research and Development
RSA	The Royal Society for the Encouragement of Arts, Manufactures & Commerce

SFI	Santa Fe Institute
SNA	System of National Accounts
TMT	Top Management Team
UN	United Nations
UNEP	United Nations Environmental Programme
UNRISD	United Nations Research Institute for Social Development
UNU	United Nations University
WANEP	West African Network for Peacebuilding
WTO	World Trade Organization

Author Biographies

Mika Aaltonen is a Ph.D. (Econ.), Adjunct Professor (Foresight & Complexity), Fellow of The Kenos Circle in Vienna, Board Member of The TimeAdventurers′ Club in Copenhagen, Editorial Board Member of the E:CO (Emergence: Complexity and Organizations) journal, Fellow of the Royal Society of Arts in London, Corresponding Member of the European Regional Foresight College in Paris, Planning Committee Member of the American Council for the United Nation′s University Millennium Project in Washington, and Confirmed Speaker of the World Future Society. He is also Head and Chairman of the Board of StraX (the research unit for strategic intelligence and exploration of futures) at Helsinki University of Technology.

Stefan Bergheim is Senior Economist at Deutsche Bank Research (DBR). He studied economics at Saarbrücken, Germany and for three years in the Ph.D. program at the University of Oregon, where he also taught international economics. He has worked for global investment banks and their institutional clients since 1995, covering the German and European economies from Frankfurt.

Since 2002 Stefan has worked for DBR, with a focus on demographics, human capital and long-run economic growth. He is the lead analyst in the DBR's ongoing megatopic Global Growth Centres. DBR is the think tank of the Deutsche Bank Group, which is based in Frankfurt. It focuses on the analysis of global economic, societal and financial-market trends, i.e. the environment in which the Deutsche Bank operates. It actively promotes public debate on economic, fiscal, labour-market and social-policy issues. Current research topics include Global Growth Centres, demographic change, China's growing economic and political status, energy (the world after the petroleum age) and Germany's return to growth.

Paul Cilliers is Professor of Philosophy at the University of Stellenbosch in South Africa. He teaches Cultural Philosophy, Deconstruction and the Philosophy of Science. He also has a degree in Electronic Engineering and worked professionally as an engineer for many years. His research is focused on the philosophical and ethical implications of complexity theory and he has published widely in the field. He is the author of *Complexity and Postmodernism* (Routledge 1998). He also has a lively interest in literature and music.

Tapio Kanninen (Ph.D., Political Science) was Chief of the Policy Planning Unit at the UN Department of Political Affairs (DPA) in New York from 1998-2005. He is currently the Head of the Unit at the DPA for Cooperation with Regional Organizations, in which function he plans the agendas, documentation and proceedings for the UN Secretary-General's annual meetings with heads of regional and other intergovernmental organizations.

A long-term UN career official, Dr. Kanninen has worked, among other things, UN reforms for the Secretary-General's Office, as a statistician in order to create a global system of environmental data in a project funded by the UNEP and as secretary of many UN reform groups, including, Security Council enlargement and the revitalization of the whole UN system under the chairmanship of the President of the General Assembly. At the beginning of the tenure of former UN Secretary-General Boutros Boutros-Ghali, he was secretary for the drafting group of An Agenda for Peace, a report requested by the Secretary-General during the first Security Council meeting at summit level in 1992. He was also the convener of an interdepartmental working group to implement the report's recommendations in conflict prevention, peace-making, peace-keeping and peace-building. From 1994 to 2005, Dr. Kanninen was also a focal point for preparing the Secretary-General's reports on New or Restored Democracies to the General Assembly. Before joining the UN he was, among other things, in charge of the preparations for a first social indicator report of Finland at the Statistical Agency of the Government, a project funded and promoted by the Prime Minister's Office.

Eve Mitleton-Kelly is Founder and Director of the Complexity Research Programme at the London School of Economics; Visiting Professor at the Open University, UK; Coordinator of Links with Business, Industry and Government of the European Complex Systems Network of Excellence, *Exystence*; Executive Coordinator of SOL-UK; and Advisor to European and US organizations. Eve Mitleton-Kelly´s recent work has concentrated on the application and the implications of the theories of complexity for organizations and specifically on strategy, IT legacy systems, organizational learning, the development of enabling environments and the design of emergent new organizational forms. She has published many papers on complexity and edited a book *Complex Systems & Evolutionary Perspectives of Organizations: The Application of Complexity Theory to Organizations* (Elsevier 2003).

T. Irene Sanders is Executive Director of the Washington Center for Complexity and Public Policy and author of *Strategic Thinking and the New Science: Planning in the Midst of Chaos, Complexity and Change* (Free Press/Simon & Schuster 1998). She pioneered the application of chaos theory and complexity in strategic thinking – the most essential skill in today's fast-paced business environment. She is easily recognized as one of the most innovative thinkers and communicators on the subjects of individual and organizational change, and leadership. She is a powerful and engaging speaker, educator and facilitator, who helps individuals and organizations see, understand and influence the dynamics of the real world context in which their decisions are being made.

Acknowledgments

Many people have influenced my thinking in recent years. Here I have the opportunity to thank those to whom that I feel most indebted. I specially would like to thank the various groups with whom I have, more or less, frequently worked with during my professional career as they have been constant sources of new ideas and inspiration.

The Kenos Circle in Vienna is a society of professional academics, business theorists, and commercial consultants who share a common interest in the concepts, tools, and methods of modern complexity science and management for understanding 'the future'. The Kenos Circle aims to create many possible worlds of the future, and explore the relative likelihood of each of them coming to pass. The society's goal is to provide the information, insights, and methods to foresee and assess future events on all time scales, ranging from relatively short-term shifts in cultural trends in popular fashion, music, and film to intermediate-term movements in political and economic activities, such as elections and demographic shifts, to long-term events such as the outbreak of wars and long-range economic and financial trends.

The people at The Kenos Circle to whom I would like to address my gratitude are John Naisbitt, John L. Casti, Harry Swain, Robert Prechter, Nebojsa Nakicenovic, Matthias Horx, Gregory Benford, Gerhard Hanappi, Guenther Koch, Keith Fitz-Gerald, Michael Zillner, Michael Loescher, Bill Sarubbi and Thomas Seifert.

'Stop linear thinking' is a phrase that comes to my mind immediately when I start to think about **E:CO** (Emergence: Complexity & Organizations). E:CO is an international and interdisciplinary conversation and a scientific journal about human organizations as complex systems and the implications of complexity science for those organizations. E:CO seeks to blend the integrity of academic inquiry with the impact of business practice, while integrating multiple perspectives in management theory, research, practice and education. In E:CO I would like to direct my greetings to Peter Allen, Jeffrey Goldstein, Dave Snowden, Michael Lissack, Max Boisot, Bill KcKelvey, Kurt Richardson, Caroline Richardson, Marshall Clemens, Pierpaolo Andriani, Elena Antonacopoulou, Hugo Letiche, Douglas Griffin, Stan Metcalfe, Paul Cilliers and Pedro Sotolongo.

This year **The American Council for the United Nations University Millennium Project celebrates its 10th anniversary. The Millennium Project** is a global participatory futures research think tank of futurists, scholars, business planners, and policy makers who work for international organizations, governments, corporations, NGOs, and universities. The Millennium Project manages a coherent and cumulative process that collects and assesses judgments from its several hundred participants to produce the annual reports and special studies.

I have had the pleasure to work with the special people involved in the Millennium Project and I like to use this opportunity to gratefully acknowledge the work of Jerome C. Glenn, Theodore J. Gordon, Elizabeth Florescu, Mohsen Bahrami, Eduardo Balbi, Eleonora Barbieri Masini, Peter Bishop, Frank Catanzaro, Paul Crake, José Cordeiro,

George Gowan, Cornelia Daheim, Fransisco Dallmeier, Nadezhna Gaponenko, John J. Gottsman, Miguel A. Gutierrez, Hazel Henderson, Arnoldo José de Hoyos Guevara, Zhouying Jin, Geci Karuri, Anandhavalli Mahadevan, Kamal Zaki Mahmoud Sheer, Shinji Matsumoto, Ruben Nelson, Pavel Novacek, Conceptión Olavarrieta, Youngsook Park, Charles Perrottet, Cristina Puentes-Markides, David Rejeski, Stanley Rosen, Mihaly Simai, Rusong Wang, Paul Werbos, Paul Wildman and Norio Yamamoto.

I have always appreciated French philosophers and sociologists. I think that there is a lot of good thinking in France, but it does not necessarily reach as wide an audience as often as it perhaps should. For that reason I have sought to get to France often and to work with their experts whenever it has been possible. My thanks are due to those French experts who have directed their efforts in making sense of and influencing the world of futures analysis. Today you can find many of them at the **European Regional Foresight College**. They are Michel Godet, Hugues de Jouvenel, Philippe Destatte, Saphia Richou, Pierre Gonod, Demosthéne Agrafiotis, Nacima Baron-Yelles, Colin Blackman, Ane Bustinduy, Stuart Candy, Paraskevas Caracostas, Riccardo Cinquegrani, Guenther Clar, Júlio Dias, Philippe Durance, Gundula English, Sylvie Esparre, Emilio Fontela, Adam Gerber, Nathalie Leroux, Pierre-Jean Lorens, Michéle Marchetti, Derek Martin, Michal Miedzinski, Riel Miller, Carina Nalerio, Erzsebet Novaky, Erik F. Överland, Jean Peyrony, Gerda Roeleveld, Fabiana Scapolo, Wendy Schultz, Karl-Heinz Steinlueller, Pascale Van Doren and Ute-Hélene Von Reibnitz.

To my friend and colleague at **Dream Company** and The **TimeAdventurers' Club** in Copenhagen, Rolf Jensen, thank you for many lively discussions and for the insights that I have derived from them.

I would like to believe that putting something like *The Third Lens* together is a huge job, but honestly I must admit to you and to myself that the ease of working with numerous, highly regarded experts from high profile organizations has been a joy beyond comparison, at least in my professional life. For me *The Third Lens* represents a true collaborative achievement. I can only hope for that it will work in a way Thomas Alva Edison has described, when he stated that putting two good ideas together will cause a third, an even better one, to emerge. Our target has been to create a phenomenon of emergence that no single component would be able to create by itself. This is rather like the billions of neurons in our heads, which are able to contribute to the creation of consciousness that remains unachievable for any single component alone. So, I must give my deepest gratitude to my colleagues Stefan Bergheim from the **Deutsche Bank Research**, Paul Cilliers from the **University of Stellenbosch**, Tapio Kanninen of the **United Nations**, Eve Mitleton-Kelly from the **London School of Economics**, and T. Irene Sanders from the **Washington Centre for Complexity and Public Policy**.

Also at the **Finland Futures Research Centre** the assistance of researchers Sofi Salonen, and Tuomo Paqvalin, produced many warmly welcomed contributions.

And finally, the support of Eija Ahola and **The Finnish Funding Agency for Technology and Innovation (TEKES)** has been crucial for finishing this book successfully.

Once again, I thank you all.

Introduction – Before This Book Was Written

While watching a sunny London from my top floor hotel window, and recalling my recent visit to the Royal Society of Arts (RSA), a number of thoughts rush into my mind and somehow I link that visit to this book. The RSA is an organization that was established in 1754 for the encouragement of arts, manufactures and commerce. Lots of things must have changed along the years, but the RSA still plays a significant role in British society, a role not so distant to its original mission. Amongst the changed things is the RSA manifesto, at the moment stated in the form of five challenges: encouraging enterprise, moving towards a zero-waste society, fostering resilient communities, developing a capable population, and advancing global citizenship. A simple manifesto like RSA's is a sense-making tool beyond comparison. It represents a huge amount of work and information; it describes how an organization sees the surrounding world and its role in it. It also describes the kinds of themes and projects the organization is interested in and rules out other themes and projects. If we want to describe a system, we have to frame it, and when framing a system the limits are determined by strategic considerations. We should not view the limits as arbitrary, they are the considerations of experience and expertise, and they affect the way we understand the world and the way we will be understood by others. (Cilliers 2005).

A phrase, that came out several times in the RSA discussions, concerning strategy and mission, was 'interest in boundaries'. How should we do the work we are supposed to? How could we best influence British society? 'Interest in boundaries' excites us, it fascinates our imagination, it promises to deliver novelty, but we are not aware of what kind of novelty, and from where it will come. We often think that a boundary is something that separates one thing from another, but the concept of a boundary becomes interesting when we start to think that instead of separating things, it is an interface that brings people and things together.

These questions bring us to another organization, whose 20th anniversary I also had the pleasure to celebrate, in London. Despite the short existence of the Santa Fe Institute (SFI), it has already obtained results that have drawn the attention of the world towards it. (E.g. Waldrop 1992, Johansson 2005). For me, the SFI's example shows that new and remarkable things still keep on happening and neither a respectable history, or vast resources are needed to succeed. The logic of change, the logic of success, has not been traditional at the SFI. Instead of keeping the experts tied to their own area of expertise, the SFI pursues emerging syntheses, between mathematics and other scientific disciplines. As a result new insights seem to have emerged organizationally as well as scientifically at the boundaries, or interfaces, between organizations, people and ideas.

Nevertheless, the RSA and the SFI are very different organizations, the previous one is old and prestigious, the latter young and fast-evolving. They arose from different times, cultures and realities. They may have similar properties, but their successes and survival must have depended on highly different factors. Organizations are not ahistorical nor are they acontextual, and they should be recognised as such and treated accordingly.

Furthermore, every large organization consists of a various number of smaller parts – individuals, teams, units – that must communicate and interact together effectively for success. The success of an organization also depends on the choices and actions of various actors outside the organization walls. One of the main reasons for writing this book has been to show the differences between different actors, times, cultures and realities, and then trying to benefit from the analysis of those asymmetries in organizations' strategic work. (Weick 1982, Beneviste 1994, Castells 1996, Arbnor and Bjerke 1997, Dervin et al. 2002).

We would perhaps like to think of an organization, at least our own, as a perfect system, but instead an organization is an imperfect system, we should say a multi-ontology system, which is continuously created and re-created through communication and action, and where degrees of order vary. In our opinion, we should add sensitiveness towards these differences of order, see sense-making and decision-making as inseparable concepts, and comprehend that every time there is sense-making there is also decision-making. I would like to suggest that in strategic work of organizations the most significant decisions concern sense-making rather than decision-making.

The Third Lens is written for 21st century strategists, people and organizations, who struggle daily with multiple co-existing ontological[1], epistemological and methodological discourses. There are two ideas that form the intellectual basis of *The Third Lens:*

1. The nature of a project, its work and the strategic landscape where the work is carried out should influence (the third lens, i.e. ontology) the two other lenses that create our understanding of the world we live in (i.e. our epistemological and methodological choices).

2. The importance of time in our analysis; especially the use of chronotopes[2], places in time, serve as reflection points for sense-making and strategic decision-making with respect to the situation where they take place as well as conceptual vehicles for managing multiple times and realities.

In *The Third Lens* the properties of business and organizational landscapes are highlighted, because we believe that if epistemological and methodological choices follow the ontological analysis, then more appropriate and effective interventions in

1 Ontology is used here to refer to assumptions and ideas we have about the very nature of the phenomena under investigation; epistemology refers to the nature of knowledge and understanding that is considered achievable; and methodology naturally refers to the tools and methods that are used or usable.

2 Chronotope is also employed in mathematics, and was introduced as part of Einstein's Theory of Relativity. It has been used in biology since 1925 when A.A. Uxtomskij presented it and in literary criticism since Mikhail Bahktin (1981) borrowed it from there.

a system become achievable. Since its beginning, management science has painted a picture of an ordered universe. This has affected management thinking and business practices. For us, it is important to rethink the properties of the landscape, as even if some things and events happen in an orderly fashion, many of them do not. If we accept the idea of a disordered universe (to whatever degree), we need to be more precise about it. We have been silently taught to think that there exist two ontologies, first there is naturally that of order, but when there is no order there is chaos, the antibody of order. Recently, perhaps at least partly because of the work done at the SFI for example in physics and biology, we have discovered a third ontology, that of complexity. In complex systems, there is order, but it is emergent, it arises from the local interaction of actors, each of whom behaves according to their own principles, logic and knowledge. Thus it is logical to say that different properties and qualities in business and organizational landscapes should lead to different responses in strategic decision-making.

The importance of time has often lacked the attention that it should have been given in sense-making and strategic decision-making discussions. We see time as the single key component that influences an organization's success; the causal factor that represents the whole idea of interconnectivity, 21st century globalization and the possibilities of the wired world. Chronotopes, as places in times, connect people and organizations from various backgrounds and realities together and open up multiple possibilities for coordinated actions.

By placing the term 'sense-making' in the headline of a book, we can be sure that it will be measured and compared with the seminal book *Sensemaking in Organizations* (1995) by Karl E. Weick, the Rensis Likert Collegiate Professor of Organization Behaviour and Psychology at the University of Michigan. That was then followed by *Making Sense of the Organization* (2001), a generic theory, built on other researchers' data, re-analysed by Weick, it is also the standard reference work from which almost all the deductive research in the field begins. (See also, Parry 2003).

The lack of primary sources has not prevented Weick postulating seven characteristics of sense-making. Weick (1995, 18) reminds us that 'the listing is more like an observer's manual or a set of raw materials for disciplined imagination than it is a tacit set of propositions to be refined and tested'. Despite his words, the seven characteristics have reached an almost canonical position in subsequent sense-making literature (Coopey et al. 1997, Ifvarsson 2000, Parry 2003, Nathan 2004):

1. *Grounded in identity construction.* The notion of self is constantly under construction in our discussions and actions. Thus sense-making is an iterative process that continually redefines our image, and others', of ourselves;

2. *Retrospective.* Sense-making is an examination of past practices in order to learn, and unlearn, things about current context;

3. *Enacting.* There is no objective environment separate from our interpretation of it. An interpretation can shape the environment more than the environment

shapes the interpretation. We act and actions become part of the environment that constrains future actions. (Daft and Weick 1984);

4. *Social.* Sense-making is a social activity. Narrative, discourse and conversation are the primary media of sense-making; organizations are networks of shared meanings;

5. *Ongoing.* Sense-making is on-going; it has no real beginning and no formal end. It never starts because it never stops. At any given time, we are in the middle of something and our ideas are constantly being updated;

6. *Focused on extracted cues.* We pay attention and extract a particular cue, then link it with some more general idea or concept that clarifies the meaning of the cue, which then alters the more general idea, and so on. (Nathan 2004);

7. *Driven by plausibility rather than accuracy.* Accuracy is less important than plausibility. Filtering, speed and embellishment outweigh accuracy. Sense-making is about narratives that are socially acceptable, pragmatic and credible rather than accurate. (Parry 2003).

Although the importance of Weick's work is undeniable, it has not fostered this work. Or perhaps it has in the way that it has raised a number of ontological questions, followed by epistemological and methodological inquiries that, if answered reasonably, could add sensitivity to the often very unreflexive use of Weick's seven sense-making characteristics.

Besides Karl Weick, there is another giant in the field of sense-making; Brenda Dervin, professor of communication at the School of Journalism and Communication Ohio State University, who in her extensive *Sense-Making, Methodology, Reader* (2002) emphasises perhaps more relevant qualities of sense-making for this book's approach in respect to Karl Weick's postulations.

1. *Sense-making assumes that both humans and reality are sometimes orderly and sometimes chaotic.* In respect to time, sense-making is not only retrospective, but also future-orientated, and it occurs at the intersection of past, present and future. In this work we are not interested in boundaries between different time horizons, but also in boundaries between people, organizations, actions and events. Sense-making is gap-bridging, because by moving across times we bridge gaps inherent in the human condition;

2. *There is a human need to create meaning.* There are many ways to make sense. Sense-making is accomplished by verbalisations that involve information, knowledge, cognition, thoughts, and conclusions. But also attitudes, beliefs, values, and emotions should be included in our considerations of the essence of sense-making; as well as intuition, memories, stories, and narratives. Sense-

making goes beyond information and knowledge societies and is always targeted at creating meaning;

3. *There are differences in experience and observation.* Sense-making is tied to specific times, places and perspectives. Sense-making is not independent of human beings but a product of human observation. While we observe and communicate reality, we simultaneously take part in the process of creating it. Therefore every sense-maker is by nature a social constructionist. The differences in understandings, experiences and practices result in differences in the sense-making of the same information or situation.

For a social scientist, theory and model building are an exhausting experience, because no theory or model can correspond to its environment. Nevertheless, we should not stop trying, because we believe that there are immense margins for improvement in our understanding concerning the mechanisms of emergence and immergence. First, models can serve as guides in exploring prospective mechanisms and constraints. Second, we can look for conditions to ensure emergence and to avoid immergence. (C.f. Holland 1998). This search is something that has been occurring in management science for quite some time, new conditions – learning (Senge 1990), knowledge (Nonaka and Takeuchi 1995) and creativity (Florida 2002), to state some of the latest research – have been continuously presented in order to anticipate and control the critical phases in the process of emergence.

Indeed, most theoretical breakthroughs occur when a fundamental mechanism that causes a phenomenon is discovered. For Clayton M. Christensen et al. (2004) a powerful anticipative theory also needs a good circumstance-based categorization scheme, i.e. the sense-making and the conclusions based on the observations and studies of a phenomena must be appropriate. Getting the categories right is vital for developing a useful theory that allows us to understand why certain actions lead to certain outcomes and others fail.

The critical questions that guide our search for the fundamental mechanisms and novel understandings of causes and causalities are:

1. Who is talking? From which perspective are the points of view being presented?

2. What issues, actors and mechanisms are considered worthy of attention? What issues, actors and mechanisms are absent in a discussion? How do we consider issues of emergence and immergence?

3. What is the relation of the subject to time? Is the concept of time involved in sense-making and decision-making discussions? How is it explicated?

4. In what kind of landscape is the sense-making assumed to have taken place? Have the qualities of the strategic landscapes been discussed?

This book is the third chapter in a series that started over four years ago with *Organizational Complexity*, which I wrote together with Adjunct Professor Auli

Keskinen of the Finnish Ministry of Environment and Professor Eve Mitleton-Kelly of the London School of Economics. The foreword was written by Professor Stuart Kauffman of the SFI.

The main propositions of the previous two chapters of the series are presented below. The first chapter of the series *Organizational Complexity* criticizes contemporary management theories and claims that, there is too little space for uncertainty as they concentrate on knowing instead of not-knowing, certainty instead of uncertainty, consensus instead of conflict. This is, because the latter things are understood as 'something bad', 'something that calls into question a manager´s competence to control a situation'. (Stacey and Griffin and Shaw 2000, Streatfield 2001, Keskinen and Aaltonen and Mitleton-Kelly 2003).

Rarely, however, it is possible to perceive and define a problem or a target carefully, then design an appropriate range of action to improve the situation, and finally select the single course of action that seems to be the best way to solve the problem or reach the target. More often than not the biggest challenge is to make sense of what is really happening, and identify those factors which success or failure consists of. Too simplistic and too linear a presentation can prevent managers from seeing what is possible and what, in turn, inhibits their ability to act efficiently, and find working solutions for real-life situations.

Contemporary management theory, and managers who act based on that, tend to simplify the management discussion and have a tendency to give and search for answers that provide absolutes. It would be more pertinent to assess those issues that are under a manager's control and, importantly, also those that are not. The result would be the gaining of a fuller understanding of how the future can evolve in institutions and in business.

In the second chapter of the series, *Complexity as a Sense-Making Framework,* my co-authors were Dr. Theodor Barth of SINTEF, Norway, Professor John L. Casti of the SFI and the Technical University of Vienna, Professor Eve Mitleton-Kelly of the London School of Economics, and Executive Director T. Irene Sanders of the Washington Centre for Complexity and Public Policy.

In *Complexity as a Sense-Making Framework,* the theory of complex adaptive systems is used to rethink some of the vital issues in organizations' everyday practices.

John L. Casti in *Would-Be-Worlds* (1997) presented the key components of complex adaptive systems and the reasons why they are an interesting subject of study. Firstly, in contrast to simple systems which tend to involve a small number of interacting actors, and also in contrast to large systems which are large enough for statistical means to be used to study them, complex systems involve a medium-sized number of actors. Secondly, the actors are intelligent and adaptive, they are rational and logical when they adapt to new information and situations. Thirdly, no single actor has access to all information and knows what all the other actors are doing. Each actor gets information from a limited number of sources, including other actors, and comes to a decision on how to act based on this local information. Hence, the 'in-between' position requires special attention.

Eve Mitleton-Kelly, prefers to use the term complex evolving systems (CES) because, she states, the systems – social, cultural, technological, organizational – are not only adapting to the emerging conditions, they are co-evolving within them. The generic characteristics of CES described by Mitleton-Kelly (2003) are:

1. *Connectivity and interdependence.* The intricate inter-connectivity of elements within the system and between it is the very reason why the behaviour of people and organizations is complex. Another relevant reason for complexity is that systems often are multi-dimensional, and all the dimensions interact and influence each other;

2. *Emergence.* Emergent properties, patterns or structures can arise from the interaction of individual elements, and create something greater than the sum of the interacting parts;

3. *Feedback.* Feedback in human systems means influences that change potential action and behaviour. In human interaction feedback is rarely straightforward and uni-direction, often there are also reciprocal and indirect influences;

4. *Self-organization.* Self-organization takes place when actors spontaneously come together to undertake an activity not directed by an external agency. That can be understood as the spontaneous emergence of order (Kauffman 1993);

5. *Co-evolution.* In human ecosystems social, cultural, technological, economic and political aspects affect both the form of organizations and the relationships and interactions between them;

6. *Far-from-equilibrium.* A key concept in CES is dissipative structures; ways in which open systems exchange energy, matter or information with their environment and which when pushed 'far-from-equilibrium' create new structures and order. A related concept is symmetry breaking, which means the breaking of the homogeneity of a current order and giving space to new patterns to emerge;

7. *The exploration of the space of possibilities.* When organizations meet a constraint they need to explore their space of possibilities and find different ways of doing things in order to survive and thrive;

8. *Path dependence.* Path dependence theory contends that decisions and choices made in the past may have long-term impacts by postponing, limiting and binding future alternatives. As much as we are path dependent, we are path

creators. We are not only adapting to our environment, we are evolving within it. (Aaltonen 2006);

9. *Historicity.* The emergent behaviour of a person is seen as the result of that person's selection of choices from among a finite set of choices as well as the past choices that shaped that person's life path;

10. *The creation of a new order.* CES can create new ways of organizing, working, thinking and being.

In many organizational strategy and development processes, it is hard to recognize when something starts and something finishes. Viewing the life and economy of organizations as being part of a co-evolutionary world is comprised of the understanding that in changing markets new competitors, as well as possible partners constantly emerge, but also that temporary competitive advantages have a limited life-cycle. New ideas will replace old ones; new products will make old products obsolete; everyone has to evolve fast just to stay in the game.

In his early works Karl Weick (1969) argues that the world becomes intelligible through our processes of 'punctuation and bracketing'. In essence previous experiences allow an actor to select certain aspects from the ongoing flow of events (punctuation) and provide frames (bracketing) that explain the world.

The idea of 'punctuation and bracketing' has drawn attention towards three issues: 1) how evidence is implicitly and explicitly extracted from the ongoing flow of events, and 2) what are the frames, lenses, or mental models (c.f. Boland and Tenkasi 1995, Griffith 1999, Hopkinson 2001) to which the evidence is attached to, 3) and how are the previous two issues joined together? The third issue is important because every time an actor is unable to place a piece of information in a context the meaning of that information is lost (Aaltonen and Barth 2005).

Concomitantly, narrativity[3] becomes an essential element of sense-making. Every time sense-making is anchored in time and space in a particular chronotope, we are able to move across time and space by bridging gaps between times, spaces, people and events. The reason why stories, or certain elaborated frameworks or theories, are considered so important is that they are capable of expressing a sequence of events connected by subject matter and related in time and of doing so in both the chronological order and the causal order of a sequence. However, by 'punctuating and bracketing' certain people and events stories can and will overestimate certain causal ties, and underestimate others.

In changing global strategic landscapes, linear developments are continuously interrupted, consciously or unconsciously, by non-linear developments, and the best practices are quickly turned into old practices. Instead of ensuring a company's future, best practices can threaten it by creating obstacles for innovation and renewal.

3 Alasdair MacIntyre (1981) states: 'Man is in his actions and practice, as well as fictions, essentially a storytelling animal.' For Walter Fisher (1987) stories play such a substantial role for people in explaining and understanding their lives that he proposes a re-conceptualisation of humankind as *Homo narrans*.

Under these conditions sense-making is becoming more critical to organizations' success than decision-making.

Consequently, how we initially define a problem, the actions we take, and the arguments we use to justify those actions are all intertwined. As a result, considering the basic questions or doubts regarding the issue at stake is a vital activity. (Mittrof 1998, McKenna and Martin-Smith 2005).

There are two strands of thought that have underpinned sense-making theory and research: cognitive and constructionist. The differences between the two approaches are minor and perhaps somewhat semantic. According to the cognitive approach sense-making draws upon the shared schemata within a social group. These schemata can be called 'cognitive frameworks', 'perception filters' or 'mental models', and through them, and the previous experiences of the sense-maker, the world is construed. The constructionist approach places more emphasis upon language and argues that situations are formed within, not only communicated through, language. Sense-making is seen as a discursive process, where the discourse defines possible selves and their associated actions. The discourse can not be simply changed by will because the participants both influence it and are influenced by it. The constructionist approach regards sense-making as an ongoing process of negotiation through which the group is formed and structured. (Watson and Chiappini 1998, Joerges and Czarniawska 1998, Hopkinson 2001).

There is the danger that after discovering complexity, and finding the fascination of the 'edge of chaos' (Kauffman 1995), later popularised as the term 'the sweet spot', we might believe that everything must be complex. We could still claim that at present most approaches in management science assume and use a single ontology, that of order. Let us not return to the use of a single ontology even that of complexity.

The third part of the series, *The Third Lens,* embraces ontological diversity and proposes it as an important and novel way for increasing organizations' resiliency and adaptability with regard to forms of improved sense-making and decision-making. The aim of this book is not to create a new management ISM, a new management fad, but to provide a strong theoretical and practical basis for improving the sense-making of global strategic landscapes and our capacity to make strategic decisions.

And, if we rethink our ideas about cause and effect relations in general, and specifically with reference to organizations' practices, we will begin to see new opportunities and to realize new possibilities that we did not see before.

Accepting the idea of ordered, complex and chaotic ontologies, and recognising that each of them requires different epistemological approaches, i.e. tools and techniques within the boundaries of an appropriate ontology, is the beginning of multi-ontology sense-making, the building up of a new paradigm for sense-making theory. Plus, it will challenge some of the basic assumptions in management science.

How to Read This Book

People who practice what they preach have always been my favourites. They have integrity, and if the issue is important, why not to apply it yourself. I think that a book should practice what it preaches, and it should be written according to the lessons it tries to deliver. There are many names for the approach taken in this book. We can call the approach transformative change, radical change or second-order change (Dunphy and Stace 1993, Amis et al. 2004, Sun and Scott 2005). The basic, common feature of such a change is the alteration of the fundamental beliefs and assumptions that govern an organization. The theories that share a kinship with the one presented in these pages describe such an activity as generative learning (Senge 1990) or double-loop learning (Argyris and Schön 1996), but the target remains the same – the alteration of fundamental beliefs and assumptions resulting in changes in individual behaviour and organizational activities.

The importance of cognitive frameworks, our fundamental beliefs and assumptions, has been attached to several activities ranging from knowledge, categories, taxonomies, cognitive structures, maps, decision-making, performance appraisal, power and strategies for leadership. (Axelrod 1976, Gioia et al. 1989, Lord and Maher 1992, Walsh 1995, Robinson 2000, Nosek 2004, Goodhew and Cammock and Hamilton 2005). *The Third Lens* is interested in sense-making and demands that the rapidly changing, digital, intangible, virtual, global strategic landscape present to managers; and managers' ability to respond them.

A second-order exercise needs to be designed so that the old cognitive framework that has been constructed by past experience and which governs an individual's intuition and the interpretation of events by acting as a cognitive filter is replaced suddenly or gradually. Those dominant beliefs and assumptions must be contradicted with information that signals the inconsistency of the current cognitive framework, and if the mismatch and cognitive discomfort between the dominant framework and the second-order one, and if the cognitive discomfort state is strong enough, then new cognitive frameworks and behavioural change can emerge. (McElroy 2000, Oswick et al. 2002, Balugon and Johnson 2004).

From what kind of information and from what kind of sources can a second-order change be potentially created? Naturally, many reports, from performance appraisals to research on inefficiencies, within an organization, and information about markets, customers and competitors outside the organization, can lead to a second-order change.

Another source of disruptive information is expert knowledge. When we address difficult issues that are not known or self-evident, we tend to rely on analysis and expert knowledge. There is a dependency on experts' opinions, a readiness to accept proposed solutions when there is a lack of meaning. This kind of action is seen as necessary to survival, because denying expert knowledge would place the decision-making process in a crisis. An expert requires experience and the acquisition of knowledge over time, plus a sophisticated set of patterns through which the world can be viewed and explained, as well as recognition from within a network of interaction, because knowledge cannot exist independently, it has to be constituted within a network.

Our conclusion from this is that managers need to pay more attention to management theory rather than paying attention to simple recipes derived from a superficial understanding of past practices in other organizations 'in the naïve belief that if a particular course of action helped other companies to succeed, it ought to help theirs too'. Plus they need to understand how the theory, even when implicit, significantly influences the way they see their environment as well as the outcomes of the strategic process. (C.f. Christensen and Raynor 2003).

To follow the concept of second-order change; the ideas, contents, and structure of *The Third Lens* have to consistently support it.

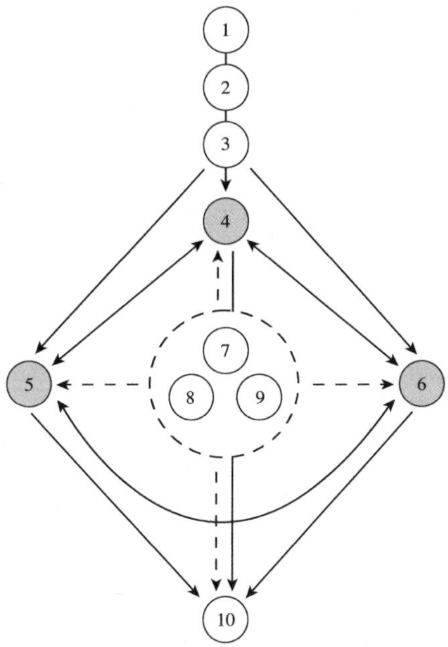

Figure 1.1 The reading map

There are four parts in *The Third Lens*. Part 1 re-sets our thoughts about strategic decision-making in the first chapter, then about sense-making in chapter two, time and the quality of the strategic landscape in chapter three. The issues are discussed thoroughly in order to prepare the setting for the following expert articles.

Part 2 offers three perspectives – economic, political and generative – for modelling sense-making. In chapter four Stefan Bergheim presents the Deutsche Bank's foresight model for evaluating long-term growth. He is the person responsible for the development of the *Formel–G* Model, and is therefore the best expert to write about it. The fifth chapter provides a systematic framework and a political early warning response system for addressing global and regional threats. It is based on the experience and expertise of Tapio Kanninen who has served successfully for a number of years in strategic positions at the United Nations. In the sixth chapter Mika Aaltonen reviews a number of societal change theories through the wise eyes of Mr. John Naisbitt in order to introduce a new generative model – 3P (Platforms, Pieces and Probabilities).

Part 3 challenges our conceptions of causality. Three perspectives, all from the leading experts on the respective perspective, are presented in order to refresh our thinking on how things emerge and immerge. Mika Aaltonen and Executive Director T. Irene Sanders from the Washington Centre for Complexity and Public Policy argue, in chapter 7, that all systems are most sensitive to the changes that take place during their initial phases and present uncertainty and asymmetry not as our opponents but as our allies in strategic management. In chapter 8, Stellenbosch University Professor Paul Cilliers presents his way of making sense of the world, which is characterised by direct and indirect feed-back loops, i.e. circular causality. And the chapter 9 is reserved for LSE Complexity Group Director Eve Mitleton-Kelly's challenging analysis of Aristotle's old concept of final cause.

Part 4 contains the concluding chapter 10 that reflects upon and assists the reader in understanding the previous chapters with regard to the presented approach – multi-ontology sense-making.

In *The Third Lens*, every chapter is able to stand alone; every chapter delivers an important piece of learning by itself. Every chapter also supports the other chapters, so that the result resembles emergence, it is something else, something more than the sum of its parts. Think of it as making mayonnaise, you add the ingredients together, stir – and, something new emerges.

This book can be read simply, like any other book, from the beginning to the end. Or you can just concentrate on a single chapter that interests you. All the chapters are suitable for this purpose. A third way to read it is to start with part 1, continue with one chapter (4, 5 or 6) that interests you from part 2, then re-evaluate it separately from the view points of other chapters in the same part, or chapters 7, 8 and 9 in part 3. And finish your reading at the end with chapter 10. If you are mostly interested in theory, then we advise you to start from part 1, skip part 2, and move straight to part 3 and the conclusions. If you are mostly interested in practical examples of how major institutes make sense of futures, then part 2 is especially for you.

PART 1
Re-setting Our Thoughts

Chapter 1

Strategic Decision-making – How It Is, and How It Used to Be

Mika Aaltonen

A recent study (McKenna and Martin-Smith 2005) shows that failure-prone tactics and a poor choice of leadership are minor reasons for the making of incorrect decisions. The major causes were found to be complexity and uncertainty in the environment that stems from two sources: 1) the nature of people's interactions, and 2) the nature of change in the environment due to changes in technology, economics, politics, demographics and other factors.

People have always been connected to responsive communicative processes within their social worlds, but today they increasingly and more easily move beyond their initial social worlds: either by networking with their natural environment (Latour 1993), or through the Internet and its technological environment (Barabasi 2002), or the weak ties of their social environment (Granovetter 1983). Due to our increasing population and improved technology, the number of connections that link people within their daily lives has exploded.

Another source of complexity and uncertainty is change in social, political and ethical behaviour. They are like strange attractors (Marion 1999) minor changes in people's values and in the ways they think about certain issues can result in unexpected changes elsewhere. Our conclusion is that, even if scientific tools and leadership style methods have their role in decision-making, their applicability is very much subjugated by a rapidly changing decision-making context.

Conventional decision-making studies are comprised of clear sequential steps: identify the problem, generate solutions, evaluate and choose from amongst the solutions, and implement the chosen solution (e.g. Cyert and March 1963, Soleberg 1967, Witte 1972, Nutt 1984). In the 1970s Henry Mintzberg (1976) argued that a linear model is inadequate for most organizational decisions, and identified cycling back and lags as well as politics and authorisation as important elements in the process. More recent approaches suggest that every strategic issue should be perceived from at least two of the four possible perspectives, which are, technical, systemic, interpersonal and existential (Mitroff 1998). Plus the identification of three stages – action, discovery and choice – in a strategic decision cycle (Stacey 1993); the application of three lenses – experience, ideas and design (Johnson and Scholes

2002); and the viewing of decision-making through three options – doing first, seeing first or thinking first (Mintzberg and Westley 2001).[1]

Stacey (ibid.) made an important finding, which is relevant to all the above mentioned theories that stress the shift away from linear decision-making approaches; he clarified that it is not possible to identify which stages comes first, a cycle may start with an action, a choice, or a discovery, and the cycle continues through time. Action may precede a decision, not merely follow it.

Why Everybody Talks About Strategy

Not to rush things too much, we must first answer the question: what is a strategic decision? Mueller, Mone and Barker (2000) state that a strategic decision has three characteristics: 1) the decision is important to the organization; 2) it involves a significant commitment of resources and/or affects the overall direction of the organization; and 3) it is representative of the type of strategic decisions that are typically made in the organization. Nutt (2000) directs our attention to organizational decision-makers and the conditions surrounding a decision. He indicates importance, urgency, internal support, and the decision-maker's level as attributes that help us to get close to the phenomenon of interest. One simple, but clever way to answer the question is to look at use of the word. When people call something strategic they emphasize the importance of their saying – and of themselves. (Holstius and Malaska 2004). In fact, according to the Oxford English Dictionary strategic actually means important.

Whose decisions, then, are important to the organization? Managers are certainly one group. However, if we evaluate the question by using other aspects, and especially, those of complex systems, then the reply goes – everybody's in the organization. If people behave according to local knowledge, their own principles, and their own rationality, they are certainly strategic from their own perspective. The second reason is that the outcome of strategic decision-making depends on many, if not all the decision-makers involved. And if an organization, a network, wants to be intelligent, all the members or nodes in it have to be intelligent too. (Fuglseth and Gronhaug 2003, Abele and Bless and Ehrhart 2004).

In addition strategy focuses on issues that are considered important, thus there are strong theoretical reasons for a positive relationship between strategic decision-making and organizational performance. Strategic decision-making encourages, by its very nature, organizations to think about long-term issues (Schwenk and Shrader 1993), provides a structured approach to the identification and evaluation of strategic options and allows the maximum use of organizational resources (Drohan 1997), and leads to the greater consistency of focus, organizational skills and organizational work effort. (Drago 1998, Cohen 2001).

In recent years, scientists, managers and experts that have attempted to understand chaos, complexity, and change and organizations trying to survive them, reached the

1 Albert Einstein insisted on looking at things from at least three different perspectives to ensure their true existence.

same conclusion: chaos, complexity and change are everywhere and mastering them requires new ways of seeing and thinking (Sanders 1998). Sound bites such as: 'We live in a time of great stirring, both natural and human made. Disruptive elements seem to be afoot, gathering strength in air masses that spiral over oceans or in decisions that swirl through the halls of power' (Wheatley 1999) have become familiar to us. Several writers (Eizenhardt 1989, D'Aveni 1994, Brown and Eizenhardt 1998, Bogner and Barr 2000, Goodhew and Cammock and Hamilton 2004) agree that for many industries rapid changes in environmental factors, the relative ease of entry and exit of firms from a business area, plus ambiguous consumer demands eliminate the potential basis for long-term competitive advantage and open the door to a wide range of potential rivals. Furthermore, emerging technologies, unexpected user patterns, and complex interactions between variables have produced unforeseeable outcomes.

Even though the depicted landscapes correspond with the ongoing developments, we must embrace ontological diversity, and note that, in addition to those kinds of landscapes, there are more ordered and more chaotic ones.

The changing strategic landscapes represent huge cognitive challenges for managers. No wonder, strategists are considered persons who have insight into the present and foresight regarding the future and are also considered to be capable of responding to changing situations and able to discriminate the different nuances in current events. Strategists also have an intellectual openness and the flexibility to entertain and address many ideas and possibilities at the same time and to select the best or most appropriate from amongst them. (Soule 2002). Decision-makers are not omniscient, though. They are constrained by a limited cognitive capacity, and are unable to know the future. (March 1994, Fulgseth and Gronhaug 2003).

To Whom Does Strategy Belong?

Classic decision-making models are set in a mostly stable and linear environment, reflecting the simpler and more stable environments of their time. They usually assume that decisions are made at the highest levels by managers who are actively involved in the running of the organization, and normally focused on one country or region. (Friedman 2000, McKenna and Martin-Smith 2005).

Departing from this background it is not a surprise that a lot of attention is given to CEOs and top managers facing strategic decisions. The top management teams (Hambrick and Mason 1984), boards of directors (Pettigrew 1992), and planning task forces (Van de Ven 1980) play a key role in strategic decision-making. A more recent development is the acknowledgement of the importance of the groups in strategic decision-making, which has led to a stream of research called organizational demographics. It is suggested that, just as individuals have a cognitive style, a characteristic way of gathering and processing information for decision-making, groups also develop a consistent cognitive style in their decision-making practices. The cognitive style of the group, or the demographics of the group, reflects differences in the composition and structure of the group, and the cognitive style and social interaction of individuals, within, but also outside the group. (Leonard et al. 2005).

Ketchen, Snow and Street (2005) identify two key characteristics in a strategy process. Participation reveals to what extent a variety of opinions is incorporated into a decision-making process. The least amount of participation includes only the CEO's opinions. However, most strategic decisions are the product of a group process that includes the views of other executives. Some decisions call for considerably more participation such as the entire top management team (TMT), mid-level managers, other professionals and outside consultants. This is a traditional, top-down view in decision-making studies, a complementary point of view to that derives from a complex systems approach, where the emergence of a situation is seen dependent on local interactions between actors. In this way the emergence of a situation, for example the success or failure of a household product depends on both the CEO's or TMT's decisions as well as on, for example, the decisions of thousands of housewives when they do their daily shopping in supermarkets. Comprehensiveness is the degree to which managers conduct exhaustive analysis during strategic decision-making. High comprehensiveness ensures a thorough consideration of the important issues but it may slow decision-making. In a multi-ontology sense-making approach, comprehensiveness becomes even more complex because first it draws our attention to the three ontologies – ordered, complex and chaotic – that recognize the nature of decision-making, then it validates tools, techniques, analysis and information within the boundaries of an appropriate ontology.

For other writers (Eisenhardt and Zbaracki 1992, Scwenk 1995, Venkatraman 2000, Talaulicar 2005) crucial indicators of the efficiency of a strategic decision-making process derive from comprehensiveness and speed. In other words, strategic decisions must be of high-quality, achieved through thorough work. At the same time, the pace of decision-making is important. Only timely decisions can lead to success. Obviously, how a TMT is organized, and what the processes among TMT members are, and how the rest of the organization influences both the comprehensiveness and pace of decision-making is crucial.

This kind of sense-making is the basis for conceiving of strategic decision-making as a means by which a TMT gathers and processes information from their internal and external sources in an effort to reduce uncertainty and to select an appropriate response. (Forbes 2005). CEOs and TMTs are also selective in their scanning, as better information is seen to increase the sense of controllability. We can talk about specially designed executive information systems (EIS) that focus on providing internal and external data for the TMT's needs. In other words, it must extract critical data, provide online reports, and meet senior executives' information needs. (Walters et al. 2003).

In *The Third Lens*, the target of a sense-making activity can be the reduction of uncertainty or the increase of controllability, but it does not have to be: depending on the strategic landscape other targets are also viable. For instance, reducing controllability in order to create space for new ideas and actions would be a purpose for it. Although the CEO/TMT standpoint is an important one, it is complemented by a complex systems standpoint. Consequently, we could talk about concepts like personal information management, not just CEO/TMT decision-making.

The Conceptual Age and the Cognitive Challenge

It has been noted that managers' sense-making and decision-making activities are tied to their cognitive frameworks or mental models. These frameworks and models are relatively abstract representations of things and events. They have developed over time through experience and interaction with others. They work in a circular fashion; when individuals interact within their environment, frameworks and models are built, reinforced and neglected, and in their turn they will be used to make sense of future interactions. Past experiences shape their template for the understanding of future experiences. (Abelson 1976, Fiske and Taylor 1991, Weick 1995, Bogner and Barr 2000).

Furthermore, cognitive frameworks or mental models influence what is noticed, the interpretation of what is noticed, and what kind of action is taken by individuals (Calambos et al. 1986). It is correct to claim that frameworks or models, like the ones presented in chapters 4, 5 and 6, play a significant role in decision-makers' sense-making. In their daily work managers are constrained not only by financial goals and constituency demands, but also by their own beliefs. (Chen and Lee 2003). Consequently, sense-making activities have a pivotal role in linking experience and knowledge to decision-making. (Hasan and Gould 2001).

Cognitive frameworks or mental models are products of, and simultaneously can produce, an interactive process of instantiation. They are based on shared assumptions, knowledge and practices. They are spread through interaction between people. They can change incrementally when they are repeatedly retold, or more rapidly through second-order change because when old frameworks and models loose their explanatory power and are no longer useful, in a sense-maker's world, they are replaced by new ones. (Bowker and Star 1999, Axelrod and Cohen 2000, Aaltonen 2005).

The path the cognitive approach takes towards knowledge is not to try to code tacit knowledge, nor to try to store, share or pattern it, but rather to understand how cognitive frameworks and mental models produce certain behaviour patterns in people, and how they create affordances for the construction and co-construction of reality by actors with different experience and knowledge. (Preziosi and Farago 2004, Jacucci 2005).

Cognitive frameworks and mental models enable individuals to make inferences and predictions. They can be represented in many forms: spatial relations between actors, temporal and causal relations among events. Chen and Lee (2003) contend that managers use the information they have collected from various internal and external sources to develop a series of frameworks and models. Moreover, when dealing with complex issues the effectiveness of a manager's decision is determined to a large extent by the quality of his or her frameworks or models, because they influence action alternatives and subsequent outcomes. A conclusion follows: 'The less you see, the less you are able to manipulate and capitalize on change'.[2]

Previous research in cognitive psychology, behavioural decision theory, and strategic decision-making identifies several cognitive simplification processes or

2 A phrase used by Michael S. Loescher, President of the Copernicus Group.

heuristics that decision-makers use when they deal with uncertainty. These processes include 1) availability, when decision-makers tend to rely on recent information or information that is easy to recall, but simultaneously they fail to envision important pathways in the emergence of the future (Russo and Schoemaker 1992); 2) adjustment and anchoring, when initial judgments about certain drivers and variables are made and new data is attributed to them, though anchoring, based on past experience may be misleading when there is a major discontinuity in a strategic landscape (Schwenk 1984); 3) prior hypothesis bias, which occurs when individuals tend to seek and use information consistent with their beliefs (Jervis 1976); 4) while reasoning by analogy involves the application of analogies from past cases and simpler situations, which helps to reduce uncertainty, unfortunately the information has often lost the context in which it originally worked (Chen and Lee 2003).

The interpretation of a stimulus situation depends on the schema that is activated and applicable to the stimulus situation (Fiske and Taylor 1991). In brief, what we understand and how we understand a situation depends on the information we bring to a given situation, and the longer we think about the situation the more its cognitive representation changes. It may be assumed that cognitive elaboration activates more schemata (Tesser 1978).

In complex systems, a heuristics does not depend only on the individual, as social interaction is likely to activate more schemata. Thus, regardless of whether we are visiting a client, having a conversation with a colleague, or attending a meeting people involved in social interaction act and react sequentially to each other. (Abele et al. 2004). Actors in a social situation move sequentially and they are interdependent, but from time to time they can also move simultaneously and still be interdependent. Ultimately, they inherently face uncertainty, when they have to make decisions and the outcome of their decisions depends on other actors' decisions, which they can not know and have limited influence upon.

Chapter 2

Making Sense of the Past, Present and Future

Mika Aaltonen

In a study (Turkle 1997) children's interaction with complex computer simulations were viewed. Faced with opaque and interactive simulation objects, characterized by 'unstable meanings' and 'emergent, evolving truths', it was found that children try to impose order making do with whatever framework or model can fit a prevailing circumstance. (Krems 1995, Lundberg 2000).

Everyone who has worked with novel and quickly developing situations is familiar with this kind of sense-making. When only the symptoms are available and causes have to be inferred, managers have to construct frameworks and models that represent the situation as extensively as possible. Often, managing only the visible layer, without seeing or understanding the hidden one, is an incomplete and only a partly helpful strategy. Other strategies that could influence the emergence and immergence of the situation would therefore be helpful.

How children deal with artificial life suggests that maintaining parallel definitions that alternate in a way that resembles rapid cycling is their form of adaptation. (Krems 1995, Turkle 1997). This kind of strategy is not perhaps far away from arguments that propose that cognitive flexibility correlates positively with expertise; changing strategic landscapes requires flexible information processing systems: multiple interpretations of information, the modification of representations, and the modification of strategies.

The Third Lens claims that in addition to a rich mental toolbox with varying levels of abstraction, the major source of organizational flexibility and effectiveness stems from the ability to make sense of the properties and dynamics of an organization's strategic landscape and the use of tools and methods accordingly.

More emphasis may be placed on making sense of the emergent processes that are not clear and visible, and trying to make clear connections between the visible and hidden layers presented in Figure 2.1.

In addition, we suggest that three forces – sensitiveness to initial conditions, circular cause and final cause (chapters 7, 8 and 9) – and the interplay between them could be comprehended as a complementary view for making sense of and managing the hidden layer, i.e. the emergent properties of the strategic landscape. (See more, Aaltonen 2006):

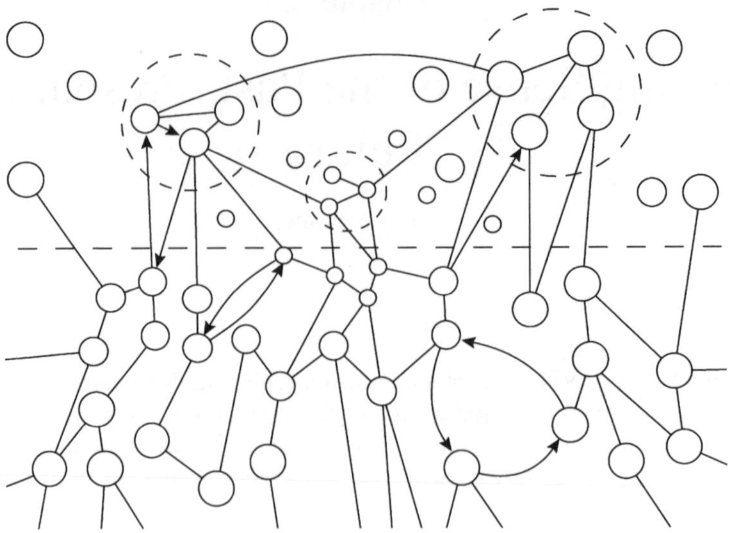

Figure 2.1 The two layers – hidden (below) and visible (above)

1. Sensitiveness to initial conditions assumes that complex systems are sensitive to the changes that take place during their initial phases. These initial phases are the points of influence for the future;

2. In a networked society, circular causality, how connectivity and feedback influence evolution, is the dominant type of causality. The conscious management of both direct and indirect feed-back loops influences emergence;

3. People's goal-seeking activities are sensitive to final conditions. Small variations in the occurrence and type of response received from larger environments can dramatically influence how and which contingencies are reframed as the context of this response in the agglomerate. (F. Barth 1992, T. Barth 2005).

Hindsight, Insight and Foresight

Managers' thought processes are considered rational, but they are also highly inferential, intuitive, opportunistic, and qualitative. In addition, their thought processes are directed backwards to understand the history, and forwards to anticipate the future, and successful managers have the capability to think back and forth between past, present and future.[1] (Chen and Lee 2003).

1 In 1642 in his doctoral thesis for the Academy of Turku Michael Wexonius wrote that knowledge has three eyes: memory when it looks back at the past, wisdom when it looks at

Hence, the ways we understand the past, come to grips with the present, and imagine the future, are extremely valuable in providing continuity and direction for our lives. Sense-making is rooted in time and space, and occurs at the intersection of three horizons: the past, present, and future. Often we talk about three different domains of knowledge related to these three time horizons – namely, hindsight, insight and foresight.

As human beings we construct, and are constructed by the different systems we live in, our networks of friends, the organizations we know, the parts of society we are engaged with et cetera. Such interaction takes place in an open process that will have passing closures through which perceiving, retrieving and enfolding effects, that are beyond the initial scope the system, occur (Shaw 1997).

The landscape where this evolutionary process takes place undergoes and sets in motion continuous change created by actors and their actions, which subsequently affects all other actors and their actions. In such conditions, the landscape has co-evolutionary features, not just its evolutionary ones. In co-evolving landscapes, the adaptive moves of one actor impact upon and change the landscapes of that actor's co-evolutionary associates.

We emphasize that sense-making asserts that a person's, a group's or an organization's understanding of a situation, rather than the situation's objective properties shapes the way that a person, group or organization acts in the situation (Czarniawska 1997, 1999). The implicit or explicit use of frameworks and models of scanning, framing and interpreting also construct a conception of the situation at hand (e.g. chapters 4, 5 and 6). In effect, sense-making, by preceding decision-making, plays a significant role in framing the range, reach and depth of forthcoming decisions (Woodside 2001).

Hindsight, insight and foresight are inseparably connected with our everyday life when routines established through past experiences are used in decision-making to support and guide it by having positive or certain expectations of it, and on the other hand when routines limit our attention and thinking. In this process, imagined futures, be they simple extrapolations of the past or wild presentations never before encountered, provide feedback that directs and regulates decision-making and affects organizational creativity and change (Ford 2001).

Path Dependent and Path Creator

Path dependence theory contends that decisions made in the past are likely to have long-term impacts by postponing, limiting and binding future alternatives. Path dependence theory has been used by economists, especially by those involved with evolutionary economic theory, but path dependence theory is also accompanied by mathematical literature on nonlinear models, chaos and complexity models, from which the term and concept of sensitiveness to initial conditions derives. (Nelson and Winter 1982, Magnusson and Ottoson 1997, Garud and Karnoa 2000).

---

the present and responsibility when it deals with the future.

Path dependence is one type of causal theory. It makes more explicit some of the vital elements of the decision-making processes through which the future is supposed to emerge. Three degrees of path dependence have been recognized: 1) there exists sensitiveness to initial conditions, but with no implied inefficiency, 2) there exists sensitiveness to initial conditions, that leads to outcomes that are costly and regrettable, 3) there exists sensitiveness to initial conditions, and there exists or has existed, some feasible arrangements for achieving the preferred outcome, but that outcome was not obtained. (Liebowitz and Margolis 1995, Aaltonen 2006).

We can move forwards and backwards along path dependence theory by using scenarios and counterfactuals. Scenarios are future-oriented as they focus on what might yet come to pass, while counterfactuals are narratives of what might have been. Scenarios and futures thinking generally, assess routes to ask what kinds of possible paths lay ahead? Counterfactuals and past-oriented thinking bring alternative history up-to-date and ask how the alternative present differs from our own. Counterfactuals are characterized by 'What if?', and 'Even if?' questions. (Bulhof 1999, Rosenfeld 2002, McCloy and Byrne 2002).

The main rule in these kinds of exercises seems to be finding a divergence point, for example a point in time that is plausible, definite, small in itself, and yet massive in consequence. (Shippey 1997, Hellekson 2000 and 2001). Harry Turtledove (2001) points out that the establishment of a historical breakpoint is only one half of thinking about alternative histories. The other half, the more interesting and difficult one, is imagining what would result from the proposed change.

In every situation there are scenarios that compete with other scenarios purportedly constituted by good reasoning. (Fisher 1987). The world can be seen as a set of stories from which we must choose the correct ones in order to live our lives in a process of positive continual re-creation. Good stories produce action, bad stories however remain negatively influential, but if sense-making is understood as an ongoing process of negotiation, the future is story-driven[2], and is driven by the best stories.

Peter Bearman, James Moody and Robert Farris (2003) ask a fundamental question of path dependence theory: 'when, if ever, do single events change history?' The meaning of a single event is always tied up to its position in a sequence of inter-related events. In building a historical story, for example looking backwards in figure 2.2, we identify some events as salient, and deny other events as not salient. History involves a selection of events that may be nothing but the placing of thin lines of interdependent causes and events, into a story. Actually, the mechanism of telling a story about past events can be stated in one sentence – the stronger the story the thinner the history – and this mechanism drives us to believe that 'butterfly effects' do drive history, which in fact is seldom the case.

The truth is impossible, or at least it often escapes us: individuals disappear into collectives, conflicts disappear into consensuses, alternatives disappear into obvious choices, accidents disappear into clear-sighted strategies, multiple events disappear into single thematic events, and the fragility of change disappears into images of

2 An expression used by the Chief Imagination Officer Rolf Jensen of the Dream Company in a conversation.

solidity. The truth is more subtle and complex than history, but allowing complexity into the rewriting of history can be a source of innovation and change. (C.f. Kanter 1983).

Scenarios and even extrapolations are plausible, and often strong, stories about the future. They are criticized for being ontologically linear, for example extrapolating the present landscape, and its causal relationships, against an unchanging background. The hard and painstaking work of bringing to people's awareness any new possible developments though would demand the rupturing of epistemological and ontological linearity. (Suvin 1979, Parrinder 2000).

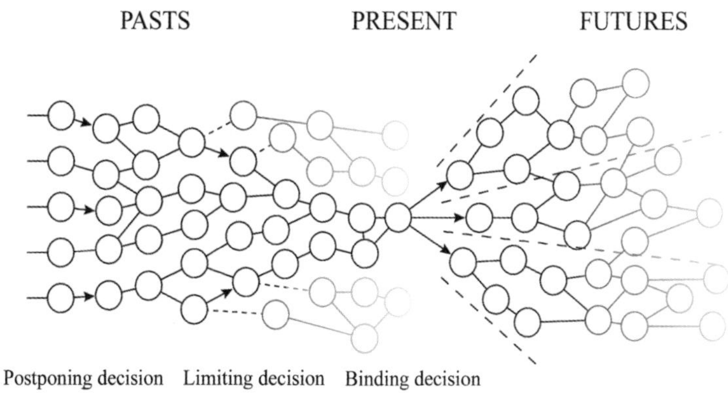

Figure 2.2 Path dependence and decision-making

Path dependence theory has also been criticized for underplaying the contingent unintended nature of outcomes from arenas of conflict and co-operation in organizations, and relying too heavily on deliberate causation (v. Wright 1986, Scarbrough 1998). This criticism has also been leveled at the extrapolation of a single element, or a few elements, that are set against an unchanging background (Suvin 1979) and the difficulties of dealing with complex chains of causality and of potentially intractable combinations of deterministic and contingent elements within actor-networks (Ayres 2000).

In evolutionary processes the next step is always the most important one, there will be no future for a system, if it does not survive from the next step nor if it endangers its own environment (c.f. Luhmann 1990). As much as we are path dependent, for example to succeed and survive our actions must fit into our environment, we are also path creators, the choosing of one path automatically postpones, limits and blocks other possible paths. In the relationship between a system and its environment, the path dependent – path creator dichotomy shows that a system has the ability to respond, as well as to be adaptive to its environment.

In social systems, the next step is always constrained, but not determined, by the particular context it is situated within. This might be considered an argument that supports the existing path dependence theory, but if at every next step it is possible that the structural properties of the social system may or may not be renegotiated, then in this kind of reflexively constructed social world, the logic, and the causal relationships and interdependencies that have constructed past success or failure, will be constantly under revision and path dependence theory could be reassessed accordingly. (C.f. Introna 2003).

If we assume that path dependence theory could be theoretically built on the epistemological and ontological assumptions conveyed, not only by sensitiveness to initial conditions, but also by circular cause and final cause, the methodological and practical consequences would be more sensitive to today's organizational planning and change management working methods and challenges.

Chapter 3

Sense-making in Relation to Time and the Strategic Landscape

Mika Aaltonen

Four Directions of Influence

In strategic work, a fundamental understanding of time and its potential treatment have received scant attention. *The Third Lens* assumes that by challenging the existing unidirectional linear concept of time more sensitiveness about continuity and discontinuity could be created. Such sensitiveness can be helpful in both ex ante and ex post sense-making when seeking multiple perspectives to draw out and engage different dimensions of time and potential paths towards the future. (Parker 2004).

Henri Bergson (1911), states that we recreate ourselves endlessly over time and mature via changes experienced in our existence. Taking Bergson's ideas a little further we could claim that any recreation can be influenced from four directions. Merely by updating our memory and changing our perceptions about the past (i.e. recognising multiple histories) we influence our present thinking. As we do by imagining our futures, and by testing and analysing possible futures with our actions.

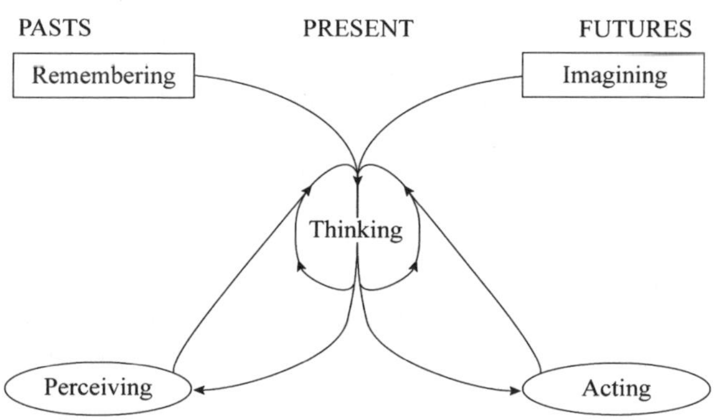

Figure 3.1 Four directions of influence

For Bergson (1911, 23) 'perception is the master of space in the exact measure in which action is the master of time'. People perceive matter and having processed those perceptions form their responsive actions. Homogeneous space and time were abstract expressions of the process of interpretation in order to determine action. This process of interpretation and action prolongs the past into the present through the exercise of memory.

History cannot automatically be equated with the past, because no history can capture the conditions, events, actors and their various relationships in the past. There is a benefit that comes with an approach that takes into account multiple histories (pasts); as they provide multiple and ever-changing representations of the past, and draw our attention towards differences in our perceptions.

The way we think about the past is an important contributor to our understanding of the present, revealing hints about the paths along which it has been formed and by placing it in a context with a changing environment. Thus we learn about the mechanisms of emergence and immergence. Furthermore through their perceptions of history, people try to distil what has been significant in their lives and activities; they learn about themselves; their identities and cultural traditions. (Hamerow 1987, Lerner 1997, Modell 1997, Parker 2004).

A few years ago an American submarine *Scorpio* disappeared on its way back home. Although the navy knew its last reported location, it could not find the missing submarine. Only after updating the knowledge on which the search operations were based was the *Scorpio* finally found, 220 yards from the place it was simulated to be situated in. (Surowiecki 2004).

The *Scorpio* example connects time to information and further to change, and gives an explicit form to circular causality.[1] It also pinpoints the importance of the accuracy of our perceptions of events in relation to our ability to act correctly and the necessity to update our memory in a cycle fast enough to deal with a changing environment.

When we make sense of the past(s), we select and connect people, events and actions in a meaningful way. As a result, we will have our interpretation of the past. But nobody owns the rights for the interpretation of any historical context. New interpretations, new presentations of causal and temporal relationships between people, events and actions, will be written intentionally and unintentionally, and they will re-examine the old perceptions and potentially influence the present by shedding new light onto our understanding of our identities and traditions. (Llewellyn 1993, Fleischman and Tyson 1997).

If we consider the world as an arena of competing stories, we might also recall that a change in the way we used to make sense of our history renders visible the previously invisible, and potentially changes the way we think, feel and act. During the time of Ayatollah Khomeini, the seeds of change were tracked in numerous mosques where the competing stories of the country's history, present and future emerged to challenge the dominant stories. These competing stories gave Iranians

1 Also a reference to Bayes's theorem is needed here. Bayes's theorem is built to calculate how new information about an event can change your preexisting expectations of the probability of the event.

new ways to think about their current situation and eventually were a cause for revolution.[2] Concomitantly, changed perceptions of the past can change the way people think and act in the present.

Hitherto we have discussed the relationships between past and present. In the following the relationships between the present and future will be discussed. The target is thus to assist in the difficult task of the anticipation of futures.[3] Many species, not only the human species, try to anticipate successful future strategies, because their survival depends on them. For the human species anticipation has been an explicit theme for centuries. For instance, the ancient Greeks presented the elements of successful strategy – action, anticipation and appropriation – in a strategic planning tool; nowadays called the Greek triangle (Godet 2001).

Weick (1995) informs us that the initial point of sense-making can also be action, i.e. an action which a person is responsible for causing. This way every person and organization chooses who or what it will be by first choosing the actions it commits to, then the actions it needs to explain, and finally the explanations it gives for these actions. In this way people and organizations choose their own constraints. A different way to understand action as a sense-making tool comes from the Dutch company Philips. At Philips strategic work consists of three time horizons (H1, H2 and H3), and the last horizon H3, more than five years from now, is continuously probed or tested with concrete prototypes.

Time and Resilience to Change

Time is certainly a complex issue. However, calling a system or a concept 'complex' does not take us very far. Niklas Luhmann (1990) would perhaps remind us, that complexity theory becomes meaningful when we are able to define and to reflect on differences, especially in a system and its environment, and the concepts of past, present and future. [4]

The interrelationships between past, present and future and re-conceptions of time serve as a means to break from the linear, unidimensional, Newtonian time based narrative. Allowing cyclical, socially constructed and spatially differentiated concepts of time into our strategic thinking serves to re-determine and re-present causation.

---

2 A story illustrated by professor Henrik Gahmberg.

3 Amongst American Indians it has been a habit that whenever an important decision is at stake, the consequences of that decision will be pondered for seven generations ahead.

4 Time-series A and B by Ellis J. McTaggart (1908) are generally considered significant in the Western tradition of thinking about time. Time-series A divides the temporal world into the past and the future, which are separated by the present moment. In time-series A, the world as a sliding duration is tied to the subjective experience of the present moment "now". Time-series B instead deals with measurable moments of time, e.g. with the help of a clock or a calendar. Time-series B represents objective time, its events are fixed with respect to time and they take place before or after a certain moment. (Bell 1997, Knuuttila 2000, Kaivo-oja et al. 2004).

Our employment of concepts of time may reveal significant possibilities for changes where previously we had detected no change, reveal parallel interdependent events where previously we had assumed none and reveal repetition of what we had thought unique. (Parker 2004). We assume that the complexities of multiple influences and impacts, spaces and time, and the co-existence of layers of time may help organizations to become more precise in their sense-making and decision-making.

Thus the theory of relativity overtakes Newton's notion of absolute time. Alternatively each person and organization has his personal measure of time depending on his own situation. As a result, a postmodernist, perhaps we should call it Foucaultian perspective on time arises, rejecting the Newtonian concept of continuous linear time along which people, events and actions travel and instead replaces it with a focus upon discontinuities and differences. In its simplest form a Foucaultian perspective denies any notion of continuity, any possible replica, between past and present. (Roth 1981, Ermarth 1992, Oldoyd 1999).

We have presentations of time as continuum and discontinuum, and there is tension in between. The Foucaultian view would not embrace an absolute or universal conception of time, and would maybe even suggest that our conception of time might derive from the interrelationships between people, events and actions, and be a dimension of them. In this way we can track emergence and immergence, continuity and discontinuity, from antecedent conditions. Continuity is generated when interrelationships emerge from past conditions while discontinuity establishes new relationships in the world. (C.f. Porter 1981).

Even in the Western tradition there are two concepts of time that are clearly separable from each other: time's arrow and time's cycle. In contrast with time's arrow, that refers more or less to an irreversible sequence of unrepeatable events that constitute a chronological order that moves in a certain direction, time's cycle posits that events are not distinct causal contributors to an end or an outcome. Rather, it conceives that events and conditions recur in simple repetitive series. Cyclical concepts of time do have an important position in people's thinking, not only in Hinduism, Buddhism and in Indian narrative cosmic cycles of repeated creation and dissolution, but also in Western thinking through the influence of Greek philosophers. (Gould 1987, Perrett 1999).

You may feel that by admitting socially constructed and spatially differentiated concepts of time, we have opened up a Pandora's box and complicated any possible understanding of determining and representing causation. I can sympathize with that feeling, but simultaneously the window for making sense of and narrating our lives has been enlarged. Challenging the linear chronology may offer us a fuller understanding of causality and change, may be helpful in revealing possibilities for changes where previously we detected no such possibilities, to reveal incremental changes where previously there had been seen only revolution, and to reveal parallel interdependencies where previously we had seen only single actors. In brief, possessing multiple perspectives about time might discover much more than we thought we knew about ourselves and our organizational lives.

The Strategic Landscape Re-discussed

In business and engineering schools in Western societies we have been taught to think, or we have been conditioned to think that order is good, something that must be maintained. If you entertain important guests and want to make a good impression, you will probably clean your table and room before their arrival, or if you want to present yourself as a competent manager you probably seek to bring things back to order as soon as they slip away from order towards chaos.

The preference for order is accompanied by the assumption that the very nature of the strategic landscape is order. In the terms of *The Third Lens*, we assume a single ontology, when instead we should assume multi-ontology.

Table 3.1 Conceptions of how the future is formed (C.f. Streatfield 2001)

In Control	Not In Control
Intended, selected, planned	Evoked, emerging
Goal, target, vision	Exploring, searching
Detecting, correcting	Amplifying
Forming	Being formed
Known	Unknown
Predictable, stable	Unpredictable, uncertain
Order, consensus	Disorder, irregular
Clarity	Confusion
Conscious	Unconscious

The way we think affects the way we act. There is nothing surprising in the strategic choices and actions that stem from traditional management thinking. If we think that way, it is only natural that we act accordingly. Shifting our thinking, or changing our perspectives would provide space for new responses, new actions. The table 3.1 does not suggest that we see the world only in terms of dichotomies, instead it suggests that by sliding from one opposite towards another you start to discover new and different solutions about the issue at stake. Maybe causing a second-order change in the way we think about our work and our world is the real work of modern managers.[5]

5 The grand old man of strategy at Shell, Arie de Gueys, puts this clearly: 'Strategic work is not about changing the strategic plans but changing the way people think about strategy'.

The two best-known examples of phase transition, or the third ontology of complexity between order and chaos, are the freezing of water and the emergence of a magnet. They both represent transitions from chaos to order. Liquid water is relatively disorganized. At freezing point it gives up this disordered state and chooses instead a state of symmetry and order. Similarly, the randomly oriented spins in a ferromagnetic metal are in a state of chaos, but they take up a highly ordered orientation once cooled under a critical temperature. (See more Barabási 2002, Watts 2003, Gladwell 2003).

The increased awareness of order at the edge of chaos has drawn the attention of experts from a wide range of fields – physicists, biologists, mathematicians and also economists. The recognition of different ontologies and the logical conclusion that follows, which is that each ontology requires a different approach to epistemology and methodology is revolutionary in its nature. In management science, a single ontology, that of order, has been tacitly accepted. If the single ontology approaches are not explicitly challenged in management practices, they will be the lens through which a situation and the solutions to improve it are viewed. They will set the boundaries to our understanding of the situation at hand, in the Wittgensteinian sense they will set the limits of our world.

Allowing multiple ontologies in the strategic puzzle, in organizations′ sense-making and strategic decision-making practices, should have serious consequences for the two other lenses – epistemology and methodology – that are constituted and constitute our everyday lives in organizations. If the three ontologies really exist, there will be tools and techniques that would be most useful within the boundaries of an appropriate ontology.

As long as people are alive and organizations exit, the strategic landscape is not stable, it undergoes and sets in motion continuous change created by actors and their actions, which subsequently affects all other actors and their actions. In a strategic process this means that not only do the actors shift position, but the landscape in which the action takes place alters too.

In his recent work Jim Collins (2001) tried to find out what makes good companies great. After careful research work, one of his conclusions was that they 'get the right people on the bus'. The conclusion is partly right, and its logic is correct, but only partly. In terms of figure 2.1, Collins's explanations work at the visible level, but they miss the causal world of the hidden level. The companies that have succeeded have had the right 'people on the bus'. The reason why that has occurred though is not properly explained and a more enlightened explanation is called for. Although it is clear that when the predictability of the future becomes extremely hazardous, even over a short period, the adaptive, self-organizing abilities of single actors become ever more vital. A co-evolutionary approach, a larger consideration of cause and effect relationships, would add that; not only does who is on the bus matter, but who is on the same road is of equal importance.

In contemporary management literature, the properties of landscapes where (organizational) dynamics happen are rarely described properly. Since its beginning, management science has painted a picture of an ordered universe, where everything is or should occur in orderly fashion. This has affected management thinking and business practices.

It is important to rethink the properties of the landscape. Even if some things and events happen in an orderly fashion, many of them do not. If the idea of a disordered universe (to whatever degree) was accepted it would, simultaneously, have serious implications for sense-making and strategic decision-making theory and practices.

If we believe that the three ontologies are significantly different due to the properties they convey, then sense-making with regard to the boundaries between the regimes becomes extremely important. This is because the dynamics of action, and therefore the action strategies should be different depending on the sense-making that is to be used with reference to the boundaries between the three ontologies. (C.f. Kaplan and Glass 1995, Juarrero 1999, Watts 2003).

We state that for social systems distinguishing between the ontologies may be approximate and the phase transition sliding.

John L. Casti (1997) provides clear criteria for distinguishing the three ontologies when he talks about the number of agents involved. Simple systems tend to have only a few interacting agents that can be carefully analysed when making sense of the system. Complex systems have a medium-sized number of agents. Hence, they cannot be as exhaustingly analysed as simple systems, and there are not enough agents to use statistical methods, thus tools and techniques appropriate for these kinds of sense-making and decision-making landscapes are required. Large systems have enough agents that we can use statistical means to study them.

Alternatively, we can look at the number of strong attractors in the system. In a very stable system there will be one or very few attractors. On the other hand in a very unstable or chaotic system there will be no strong attractors. The best place for an organization lies in neither of these. If it is too stable, it is threatened by stagnation, and if it only behaves chaotically, it is useless and inefficient. Paul Cilliers (1998) points out that for an organization a movement from one stable state to another with the least amount of effort is most likely to happen when it is (whenever possible) poised at the point of criticality, for example in between only a few strong attractors and no strong attractors at all.

The reason why we insist on figuring out these ontological boundaries is fundamental to our approach. We claim that the quality of how we perceive and make sense of situations in order to make strategic decisions depends on our ability and sensitiveness in understanding the appropriate boundaries and applying epistemological and methodological tools and techniques accordingly.

Dave Snowden (2005), Founder and Chief Scientific Officer of Cognitive Edge, states the acceptance of ontological diversity can improve decision-making in two significant ways:

1. In a crisis situation, the opportunity to move from chaos not only directly to order (and in many cases that is the target) by imposing it, but perhaps in some cases to complexity may offer a more adaptive response to the situation and the way to a more sustainable future.

2. Regular and well-motivated shifts, using for example tests and pilots, from order to complexity can prevent various forms of complacency, reduce the

possibility of catastrophic failure and be a necessary basis for organizational renewal.

For many experts and practitioners, the discovery of the third ontology, namely that of complexity, has changed their worlds. After that discovery they have put on their complexity lenses, and have begun to see complexity everywhere. This is merely the replacing of an old hat with a new one, replacing the ordered logic of interpretation with complex logic.

The Third Lens recognizes ontological diversity, the existence of not only that of the recently discovered complex regime, but also those of the ordered and chaotic that have intrigued our thinking for ages.

Chronotope Space – Linking Time and Strategic Landscape

According to complex systems logic, people are intelligent, rational and adaptive according to their respective positions and they act based on limited local information. Hence, people in the same organization, but in different positions and levels do not share the same time frame, or the same conception of the strategic landscape being considered. It is difficult, and almost certainly not beneficial, to apply a single reference time inside an organization, because of the diversity of tasks and situations, people are in.

Organizations can be seen as a continuous and intertwined flow of tactical, strategic and visionary decisions, and their modifications to situational opportunities and challenges. As time horizons would vary from the tactical that barely surpasses one year (low in figures 3.2 and 3.3), to medium-distance management and further to long or very long time horizon visionary management (high in figures 3.2 and 3.3), the characteristics of decision-making should also vary. (Wilson 2003, Holstius and Malaska 2004).

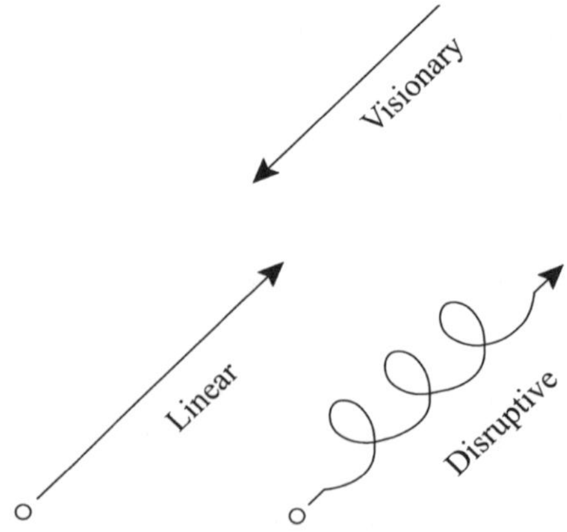

Figure 3.2 Linear, visionary and disruptive thinking

Linear thinking is focused on developing existing practices and businesses. Though it may look further into the future, it is still bounded by existing resources and is involved in allocating them properly. In contrast visionary thinking shifts the perspective, studies the present from the future and by doing that introduces a new dimension into management thinking.

In visionary thinking, we move far into the future from the present moment, and thus more things may become possible for us to envision, new insights and also non-linearities and discontinuities, for sense-making and strategic decision-making emerge. We are no longer trapped with our present means and resources and while looking at the present from the future we may consider how to prepare ourselves for futures that are assumed to include discontinuities, in the positive and negative sense of the word, and how to be proactive towards the changes that are beneficial to our targets and strategies.[6]

When we move from left to right in figures 3.2 and 3.3 the idea of a disordered universe is embedded, as we move from a linear to a disruptive world the degrees of order will vary. In the linear world there is order, in the disruptive world order is undone.

Between these two dimensions, order and disruption, we discuss linearity and non-linearity, continuity and discontinuity - the time before and the time after an intervention, whether things continue as they used to or not. Disruptive thinking presents a world more open to the new beginnings and developments, where new properties appear or disappear over the course of organizational development.

The differences between linear, visionary and disruptive thinking are depicted in figure 3.2.

At this stage it is necessary to discuss the concept of a chronotope[7]. A chronotope shows the complex trade-offs between the properties of the strategic landscape and the time frame being considered. It is the place where the knots of narratives are tied and untied: a place in time that can be constructed on one level of reality or as a combination of many levels of realities. We may talk about terrestrial or physical worlds, virtual worlds of networks and connectivity, spectral worlds of sensing and frequency management, the world of satellites and space platforms, and last but not least the social and psychological worlds that reflect the hearts and minds of people (See Loescher et al. 2000).

While moving from order towards chaos, in figures 3.2 and 3.3 from left to right, we move from known strategic landscapes, where the means and resources are more or less fixed, towards more unpredictable strategic landscapes characterized by discontinuity. Much of business development and organization development takes place in known or knowable landscapes, and actually reinforces or improves the

---

6 Nokia's change management programme is by nature visionary. It evaluates the forthcoming changes in the company's strategies and strategic landscapes, and prepares its employees with the new skills, abilities and business frames to face them.

7 In the traditional, literary definition of chronotope, spatial and temporal indicators are fused into one thought-out, concrete whole. Time thickens and becomes visible; space becomes responsive to the movements of time, plot and history. The intersection of axes and the fusion of indicators characterise a chronotope. (Bahktin 1981).

existing practices of doing business and working, but moving towards chaos gives room to disrupt, to explore ways of doing business and working that do not exist yet.

We can improve our sense-making and strategic decision-making with a more thorough understanding of time. Shifting perspectives between the actors involved in a situation and their respective ideas about time can be helpful for breaking out of the uniform concept of time, add sensitivity to socially and situationally constructed worlds and open up new tactical and strategic possibilities. In figure 3.3 the chronotope idea is used:

1. To reflect the qualities of a strategic landscape and our epistemological and methodological responses to it;

2. As an instrument for organizing people and events with respect to different times and realities.

At any chronotope we should be able to make sense of the questions or problems raised and accompany them with revised understandings, followed by the epistemological and methodological implications they convey.

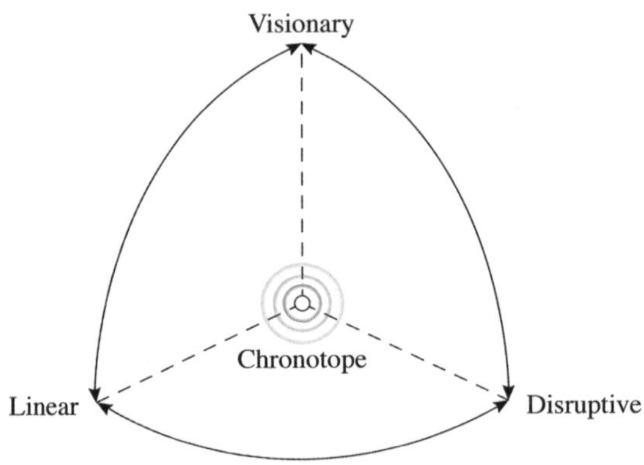

Figure 3.3 The chronotope space

A chronotope, built at any level of reality, is a possible place for interconnecting people, organizations, ideas, knowledge, expertise and events. It is also a strong vehicle for power and strategy, because it expresses the inseparability of time and space; time is seen here as the fourth dimension of space. It also functions as primary means for materializing time in space, and furthermore the use of it places people in history and conceptualises both the people and elements involved in events at that point in time. (Bahktin 1981, Bergland 1994, Gilmore 1994, Harden 2000).

Applying Chronotope Space

In the chronotope space, sliding phase transitions take place inside a defined area. Increased flexibility, in comparison with boundaries in mathematical and physical worlds, is created by off-setting rigidity in the boundaries of the sense-making process (c.f. Adner and Levinthal 2004). In the left corner where the arrows meet in figure 3.4, there is the present moment in its most stable phase. There the cause and effect relations are repeatable, i.e. certain tasks occur over and over again and are predictable, e.g. at the beginning of a new day we know what kind of a day awaits us. Here the use of hindsight is most valid. There is a wide range of appropriate methods valid and developed for this space and they derive from process re-engineering, quality management, standard operating procedures and knowledge management approaches.

In the right corner, where disruption is shown taking place in the present moment, there is chaos. There is no perceivable relationship between cause and effect, we can not know beforehand what kinds of decisions or solutions will work and afterwards we cannot be sure what led to change. Even though traditional methods, based on crisis management literature are applied.

In the top corner, where the arrows meet, is a place in the future, far distant from the present moment. The higher we move from the bottom, the further we move forwards in time. When at the bottom we talk about the present moment, at the top we could be e.g. talking about the year 2020. Various forecasting methods, impact analysis, scenario and Delphi techniques are used in this context. (Glenn and Gordon 2003).

If we take a position a bit higher and on the left side from the left corner (see left side figure 3.4), there are relationships between cause and effect that repeat, and they are still discoverable but they are no longer as self-evident as they were before. Action research, dialogue processing, causal layered analysis, and participatory methods are amongst the most preferred methods of analysis in this case.

If we now move higher and more to right (see right side of figure 3.4), we move further forward in time and the amount of uncertainty increases; the cause and effect become more difficult to discover and in fact can only be made sense of retrospectively and may not be repeatable. (C.f. Kurtz and Snowden 2003). The focus of intervention thus moves towards the hidden layer (see figure 2.1) and narrative methods, perspective filters, multi-ontology sense-making and network management are recommended for looking at this place in the future.

Chapters 4, 5 and 6 could also be placed in the chronotope space. They all have their respective positions; due to the difference of issues and perspectives they represent. Therefore a variety of insights about the future, and the tools and techniques used and developed to make sense of it, are presented.

When issues and decisions are familiar and close to certainty, cause and effect relationships are agreed on, they are linear and (relatively) simple. In situations of high agreement, there is a consensus about how people make sense of a situation and what they should do about it. When uncertainty increases, agreement on cause and effect relationships usually changes into disagreement. People move further apart in their sense-making and strategic decision-making. At this point the strategy and behaviour of a company becomes unpredictable. (See, Stacey 1996).

When organizations operate at or near equilibrium, the perceptions of boundaries are shared and people know what they are expected to do. At some point, an organization is thrown or throws itself into a state that is far from equilibrium. In this state, the old order does not seem to work anymore, there is less predictability within the environment, and in the cause and effect relationships, as well as more ambiguity in sense-making. In the zone of complexity, between linear and disruptive landscapes, the possibilities for new decisions and disruptive strategies are open. (Goldstein 1994, Kauffman 1995, Zimmerman et al. 2001, Eoyang 2003, Eoyang 2004).

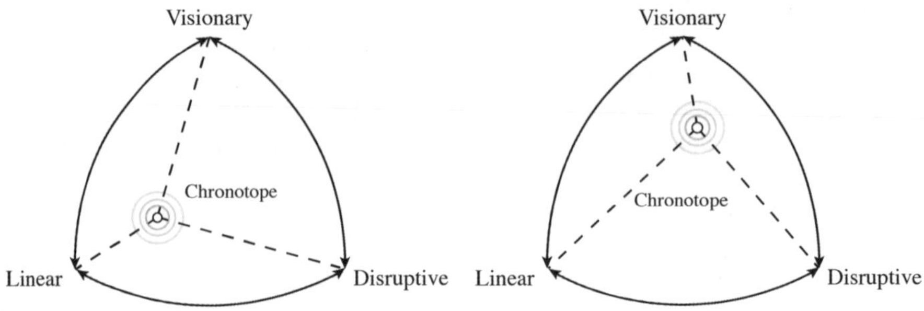

Figure 3.4 Applying chronotope space

The first way to use chronotope space is to use it as a sense-making vehicle. This starts by placing the chronotope in an approximate position in the chronotope space. The questions that need to be asked are: from which perspective or perspectives is the issue viewed (c.f. chapters 4, 5 and 6); what influences the emergence and immergence of the issue (c.f. chapters 7, 8 and 8), what is the relationship of the issue to time, and what are the properties of strategic landscapes in question (chapter 3)?

These questions should enable you to position yourself in the framework, and continue your work by making sense of the tools and methods most suited, in the approximate areas beside the chronotopes in figure 3.4, to your purpose.

The second way to use chronotopes is to use them to manage people and events at different levels of realities. That can be done because chronotopes provide boundaries, and boundaries provide a simple way of aggregating people into layers as well as constraining people's interaction. People can only interact with people who belong at the same boundary, i.e. people who use or are allowed to use the chronotope, and who can therefore participate in the action.

PART 2
Modelling Sense-making

Chapter 4

A Foresight Model for Evaluating Long-term Growth: *Formel-G*

Stefan Bergheim

Introduction

Deutsche Bank Research (DBR) is the think tank of the Deutsche Bank Group and is mandated to improve the bank's understanding of the environment it works in by feeding foresight knowledge into the decision making process. In addition, DBR's work helps internal and external customers filter incoming information, assess the importance of current events and evaluate the sustainability of observed changes in their environment. Our corporate customers look for support in detecting the geographical origin of their future customers, competitors and suppliers. An example of this work is the *Formel-G,* Foresight Model for Evaluating Long-term Growth, which will be presented in this chapter.

Demand for substantiated long-term growth forecasts is high following several unexpected developments over the past decade. The 1997 crisis in emerging Asian economies caught many investors by surprise – who wished they had been better able to anticipate the difficulties. Even worse, after retreating from Asia during the crisis, many companies were surprised by the rapid rebound of countries like South Korea and Malaysia – and wished they had had a framework that would have told them to stay in those countries. In developed countries, Germany is a case where trend GDP growth has been overestimated significantly for the past 10 years. From about 2 per cent in 1995 the consensus forecast for trend growth was revised down to around 1 per cent by 2005. Downward revisions of business cycle forecasts were the rule rather than the exception for investors and companies over these years. If they had known in the mid-1990s just how low Germany's growth potential was, some investment plans would have turned out quite different. Furthermore, policymakers are interested in specific advice on how to strengthen their countries' growth performance – or to prepare for geopolitical changes resulting from diverging economic outcomes. A systematic analytical framework and a set of conditional forecasts for growth would make their tasks easier.

While demand is strong, there is a scarcity of substantiated long-run growth forecasts. Many models simply extrapolate the past trend of GDP growth or of labour productivity into the future. Academic research into economic growth shies away from exploring the forecasting performance of growth models and focuses mostly on explaining the past. Private institutions either make ad-hoc assumptions on future growth or generate models that may not deliver what they claim to.

International organizations like the IMF have made systematic forecast errors for several advanced economies over the past years, probably as a result of incorrect estimates for potential GDP growth.

The DBR's *Formel-G* bridges this gap between demand and supply for long-run growth models.[1] It provides conditional point forecasts for GDP growth in 32 countries around the world and – importantly – a systematic framework to analyse economic growth. To this end, it combines quantitative and qualitative elements. It also links the expertise from trend researchers with that from a large number of country analysts. The framework was developed by an interdisciplinary team involving economists, a physicist and a sociologist. One of its strengths is that lessons from the history of other countries can be taken into account, as can new developments in their country-specific intensities.

On the way to formulating a model, many decisions have to be taken. These include the forecast horizon, the set of countries to be analysed, the theoretical basis, the choice of data, the econometric technique the choice of trends that are relevant for growth and assumptions on how fast these trends will develop in the future. This chapter outlines those choices and the reasons for the decisions taken. The model produces two sets of point forecasts: one set where the future is expected to evolve just as it did in the past and one that takes the impact of expected structural changes into account.

In the first step we identified the most important fundamental drivers of growth with the help of modern growth theory and state-of-the-art econometric techniques. Four drivers were selected for our model out of the large number of candidates as outlined in the fourth section (dealing with the four drivers of growth in *Formel-G*) of this chapter: population growth, the investment ratio, human capital and trade openness. The first exhibit shows how the econometric equation (described in the fifth section, 'The Empirical Growth Model') links changes in the four drivers to GDP growth.

In the second step we generated forecasts for these drivers until 2020 which were then fed into the empirical model. To ensure the high quality of these forecasts and to capture structural breaks we underpinned them with a broad-based qualitative trend analysis. We analysed the reciprocal effects among a large number of trends and used this information to group them into six coherent trend clusters as described in the seventh section of this chapter. Then we assessed the past and likely future speed of each trend cluster in our country sample. The six trend clusters of our trend map – and their link to the growth drivers – are depicted in the lower part of the exhibit and in the eighth section (The Six Trend Clusters).

1 The model was first presented in Bergheim (2005): Global Growth Centres 2020. DBR Current Issues, March 2005, which is available at <www.dbresearch.com>. Additional studies explore elements of the model in depth and provide more details of specific countries.

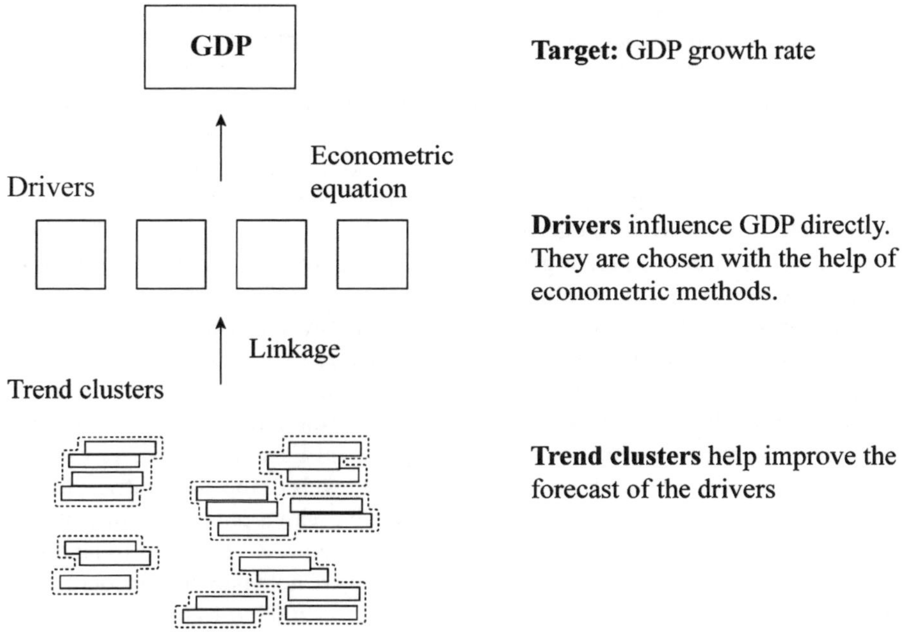

Figure 4.1 DBR's analytical framework for long-term growth forecasts: *Formel-G*

The model forecasts therefore have a broad and solid foundation.[2] However, they are based on assumptions and are subject to the usual limitations of long-term forecasts: assumptions may prove to be wrong and correlations between growth drivers and GDP (regression coefficients) might change. In particular, countries could tackle more (or fewer) reforms than assumed, which could lead actual growth to diverge from the model forecast. After all, our analytical framework not only offers a checklist for investors but also a to-do list for economic policy makers on how to achieve a better growth performance than suggested by our model forecast. Therefore, we plan to review the assumptions and trend assessments on a regular basis.

The Subject of Analysis: GDP Growth in 34 Countries

The *Formel-G* framework focuses on real GDP with its overall and per capita growth rates until 2020. Of course, GDP is not an ideal yardstick for the wellbeing of the citizens in the various countries, because part of the income generated domestically does not benefit people there but goes to foreign capital owners. In Ireland for

2 Unfortunately, this approach does not allow any out-of-sample tests of the model which would estimate the model until 1990 and then compare the forecast until 2003 with actual GDP. Data are not available in sufficient time series, and our powers of imagination required for a trend analysis starting from 1990 are too limited.

example, gross national income was more than 17 per cent below GDP in 2003. Furthermore, leisure, social stability, a clean environment and high life expectancy contribute to individuals' wellbeing – but they are not included in GDP. Nevertheless, for companies, banks and investors GDP will remain the relevant yardstick for market activities.

To ensure the comparability of GDP levels across countries we converted them with purchasing power parity exchange rates into 1995 US dollars. Differences in price levels are thus stripped out, but GDP growth rates are not affected. The focus of the analysis is thus on GDP growth overall (market size) and GDP growth per capita (prosperity). In the econometric estimate we use GDP per capita of the 15 to 64 age group as the best yardstick of productivity available for all countries; the other variables are calculated with the help of population figures.

The size of a country and the availability of data were important criteria for the selection of the 34 countries in our model. For example, there are no sufficient time series for the transition countries of Central and Eastern Europe, so we were unable to take them on board. The size and income levels of the 34 countries diverge strongly: the spectrum ranges from China and India with a population of currently 1.3 billion and 1.1 billion to small countries such as New Zealand and Ireland with a population of 4 million each – smaller countries were not taken into account. GDP per capita and year ranged from USD 2,340 in India in 2002 to 14 times that level in the USA in terms of 1995 purchasing power parities. For the emerging markets, their heterogeneity and frequent crises in the past evidently make forecasts even more difficult than for the more stable OECD countries. For two countries (Russia and South Africa) only parts of the model are available but no overall forecasts.

The Theoretical Foundation: a Production Function

Growth forecasts must have a solid theoretical foundation. The basis of most growth analyses is the neoclassical production function in which output Y is a function of labour input L, capital input K and the level of technology A (Solow residual; usually called 'total factor productivity'). Growth decompositions divide actual growth into these three components. However, over the long-term, the sole driver of any growth of per capita output is the progress of technology A. It also is crucial for the long-term increase in the capital stock per capita. Therefore, forecasts of economic growth with the help of simple growth decompositions require more or less arbitrary assumptions on technological progress. They do not explain the really interesting variable A but bury it in an assumption. Therefore, simple growth decompositions are not suitable for forecasting.

The often assumed absolute convergence of income levels between countries (for example poor countries' GDP grows faster than rich countries') also lacks theoretical and empirical support. There is no automatism: higher income levels do not fall from heaven like manna but require hard work. The GDP of a country only converges to the country-specific income level that is determined by that country's growth drivers.

Therefore, any useful model of the future has to be able to explain technological progress. This is easier said than done, however. Mankiw, Romer and Weil made a ground breaking contribution in 1992 by incorporating human capital H as a measure for the quality of labour input into the empirical growth analysis. Human capital describes a person's ability to produce output efficiently and to develop new products. This important additional variable helped significantly in explaining historic income differences across countries.

For empirical growth analysis, this was a giant step forward but not fully satisfactory. Both the theoretical and empirical work of the last ten years has tried to model the remaining, unexplained share of technological change after human capital is taken into consideration. The objective is to explain economic growth as fully as possible in the model by incorporating a further policy variable P (or several variables). Remaining exogenous, unexplainable influences are to be minimised.

show production function

$$Y_t = K^{\alpha}_t \cdot H^{\beta}_t \cdot (P_t \cdot \hat{A}_t \cdot L_t)^{1-\alpha-\beta}$$

The search for P gave rise to a flourishing literature dealing with the role of politics, institutions, knowledge and innovation. In their overview, Durlauf, Johnson and Temple (2004) identify 42 'growth theories' using a total of 102 variables – which may be combined in different variations. Although the theory does not produce a clear conclusion on the 'correct' growth model (the 'correct' P) it helps us identify potential growth drivers. The decision as to which additional variables really have a statistically and economically significant link with growth will have to be based on econometric analysis.

The Four Drivers of Growth in *Formel-G*

To be incorporated in *Formel-G*, a driver – as outlined above – must have a solid theoretical and empirical relationship with GDP growth. Population growth, investment, human capital and trade openness meet these criteria and are described in more detail in this section. Other candidate variables did not make it into *Formel-G* for various reasons: either they did not add much new information beyond our four drivers, or the econometric relationship to the growth rate was not clear, or there was not enough historical data.

Population Growth: Quantity of Labour Input

In a large number of our selected countries, population growth accounts for roughly one-third of total future GDP growth and is thus one of the most important fundamental drivers of growth: a rise in labour input also leads to higher GDP overall. Of course, this is of secondary importance for the individual citizen. In the first step, our empirical model estimates the GDP growth per capita of the 15 to 64 age group as our measure of productivity. With the help of our population forecasts, all other variables are deduced.

For the historical population development (overall and of the 15 to 64 age group) we use data from the Groningen Growth and Development Centre and the World Bank's World Development Indicators. For the baseline forecast, we use the interpolated UN population growth forecasts of 2002. Certainly, a better measure of actual labour input would be hours worked, which would also account for differences in participation rates and retirement ages. These variables have to be closely monitored in any country analysis, but unfortunately they are not available for all countries in our group.

According to the theoretical model, an increase in a population initially leads to lower GDP per capita as the existing capital stock has to be distributed across a larger number of workers. By contrast, the long-term relationship in our regression equation seems to point more to a demographic function: high-income countries tend to have lower birth rates and lower population growth.

Investment Ratio: Accumulation of Capital

One of the classic drivers of growth is the investment ratio, which determines the accumulation of physical capital. It is included in every theoretical and empirical model even though the investment ratio cannot rise forever and in view of declining marginal returns does not allow higher GDP growth per capita but only a higher GDP level in the long run. Furthermore, empirical analyses suffer from endogeneity problems: investment is a function of economic growth in the short run and a function of technological progress in the long run – i.e. the other variables in our model.

For the OECD economies, we use the share of the real investment of the corporate sector in real GDP taken from the OECD database. This data is not available for the emerging markets. Therefore we use the share of total investment in real GDP for these countries from the World Bank's database. Over the past decades, investment (or its ultimate determinants) played a major role for economic growth, especially in South Korea and Germany. In South Korea the investment ratio rose from 5 per cent of GDP in the early 1960s to over 35 per cent in the early 1990s. By contrast, in Germany it fell from 25 per cent at the beginning of the 1960s to below 15 per cent in 2002. However, as indicated earlier, investment ratios usually do not have a long-term time trend, and therefore can only have a medium-term impact on growth. Our forecasts for the investment ratios therefore make use of the fact that investment ratios only briefly move outside the range between 15 per cent and 30 per cent. In South Korea, the investment ratio has meanwhile fallen back to 25 per cent.

Human Capital: Quality of Labour Input

The human brain is a major source of wealth and growth. Non-economists often have reservations with regard to the concept of human capital – on the grounds that human beings are only seen under the aspect of economic benefit. However, the importance of education has been recognised and accepted all over the world. Human capital stands for the quality of labour input, the ability to combine production factors efficiently and the capacity to absorb and apply new knowledge and to pass it on. This accounts for a major share of technological progress.

The best available yardstick for human capital is the average number of years of education per capita of the 25 to 64 age group, which the OECD calculated back in 2002 for 95 countries for the past and up to 2010. This measure takes into account university level education but does not include professional training. According to this definition, Germany (13.5 years), Switzerland (12.9 years) und Canada (12.9 years) had very high levels of human capital in 1998; China (5.8 years) and India (4.1 years) ranked at the lower end. From 1988 to 1998, Italy, Spain and South Africa made a particularly great leap forward of more than 1 ½ years each. By contrast, almost no progress was registered in the US, Denmark and recently Germany. Since we look at the average stock of the human capital of the 25 to 64 age group, the number of years of education shows a rather stable development. This greatly facilitates forecasts.

Of course, our measure of human capital is not a perfect measure. For example, years of education in different countries may be of a different quality. However, the years of education are usually positively correlated with quality measures such as those from the Programme for International Student Assessment (PISA). The mathematical proficiency of today's pupils according to the PISA programme 2000 and the average years of education of the working-age population have a correlation coefficient of 0.67. This positive correlation between the quantity and quality of human capital is likely to also hold for those of working-age today. Another caveat is that education years do not factor in experience and life-long learning. However, these have probably been of minor importance so far and may also correlate positively with the number of years of education. Another complicating aspect is that human capital probably improves also when the number of education years stays the same but the teaching methods and curricula develop positively and the latest academic findings are imparted.

For our GDP forecasts we use average years of education as the best available proxy for human capital and we also factor professional training into the forecast, which will not be taken into account in the officially recorded number of education years.

The empirical correlation between education and income is clearly positive. Microeconomic analyses regularly explain much of the difference in income between people with differences in their levels of education. What applies to individuals also applies to entire economies: Our panel estimate finds a statistically significant relationship between the level of human capital and the level of GDP for both the OECD countries and the emerging markets. The size of the coefficient is consistent with estimates generated by the OECD: in the long run a 10 per cent increase in the number of years of education results in an 8 per cent increase in per capita GDP in the OECD countries and a 9 per cent increase in the emerging markets. In Germany, 10 per cent would today translate to an additional 1.4 years and in China to 0.6 years. In our model, human capital – along with openness – is the key driver of economic growth over the long run. As part of the DBR's megatopic 'Global growth centres', Bergheim (2005b) covers human capital and its past and future evolution in the 34 countries in more detail.

Trade Openness Promotes Learning

If a country trades more with other countries, then the competitive pressure on companies and the state increases, leading to efficiency gains and a higher production potential. In addition, the country can benefit from the technological progress embodied in imported capital goods. Economies of scale in production may be realised. With the same amount of human capital (as defined above) more output can be produced. In standard neoclassical models of comparative advantage trade increases the consumption possibilities of the population, but real GDP does not grow as the production potential of the economy does not change.

Our measure of the openness of a country is based on the average of the shares of imports and exports in the gross domestic product. We adjust this foreign trade share using purchasing power parity exchange rates in order to correct for the differences between the domestic price level of non-tradable goods and the world market prices of exports and imports. With the exceptionally high domestic price level in Japan the country's national accounts, for example, report a lower foreign trade share than at the average prices of the other countries. The exact opposite can be observed in China, where domestic prices are still relatively low. Since small countries conduct more foreign trade than large countries we make a further adjustment to the purchasing power parity of the foreign trade share by using the size of the country's population.

Trade openness as measured with our approach has been on an upward trend for all countries during recent decades. The most open economies in 2002 were Germany, Belgium, the Netherlands and France – all in the heart of Europe and founding members of the EU. The most closed economies were Argentina, South Africa and New Zealand. Mexico, India and Turkey have opened their economies extremely rapidly during the last 10 years. Among the OECD countries Spain and Ireland have opened up particularly fast.

Our empirical analysis finds a significant positive link between the degree of openness and the level of GDP, with the coefficient in the OECD countries more than twice as high as that in the emerging markets.

Other measures of openness take into account capital mobility (e.g. direct investment), the level of tariffs or non-tariff trade barriers. However, in our view these measures are less suitable for a growth model than our openness measure as they do not capture the bilateral relationship with other countries as accurately. Many of the other measures also show a significant positive correlation with our measure. Neuhaus (2005) covers the different aspects of openness and its past and future evolution in the 34 countries in more detail.

Not Included: Research and Development Spending

Apart from these four drivers there are, as mentioned above, dozens of other drivers of growth used in an empirical analysis. For a variety of reasons they have, however, not made it into our empirical model. Nevertheless, we will discuss some of them briefly here: Spending on research and development (R&D) is an obvious candidate to explain technological progress. However, it does not make it into our model because it is positively correlated with human capital, and because long-term time series are not available. With the outliers being Finland and Sweden high R&D spending as a percentage of GDP is accompanied by a high level of human capital. For these countries time series data on R&D spending would probably yield only minimal additional information. It is hardly a surprise that spending on both R&D and education are goals of the EU's Lisbon agenda.

In addition, openness can be a partial substitute for domestic R&D spending: Via trade or direct investment a country can gain access to technology from abroad. There is a global knowledge base, which disseminates knowledge more quickly with today′s improved information technologies. However, the user country must also be in a position to apply this knowledge by first investing in education itself.

The Empirical Growth Model

In parallel with growth theory, econometric analysis has made great progress in the last few years. Better and more comprehensive datasets for ever longer periods have become available and econometric techniques have been considerably improved. The state-of-the-art technique these days is panel regressions even though cross-section regressions continue to be very popular. In cross-section regressions average annual GDP growth from 1990 to 2000, for example, is explained by the initial level of income in 1990 and the averages of other variables from 1990 to 2000 on (for example institutions, openness, inflation, investment and so on).

However, the cross-section analysis does not take into account information embedded in the series' time dimension. Therefore we applied a modern panel procedure using annual observations of the various growth drivers in the 32 economies of our group. The first efforts to generate growth forecasts with the help of panel regressions were regressions which (with the exception of the constant) estimate the equal slope coefficients of the variables for all countries (fixed effects). As these assumptions are very restrictive, the alternative approach estimated separate equations for each country and then calculated the averages of the respective slope coefficients (mean group). However, because of the limited number of observations for each country, this procedure is inefficient. The pooled mean group technique is a compromise method which assumes the same long-run relationship between the (log) levels of the growth drivers and (log) GDP per capita in all countries but allows country-specific convergence coefficients, constants and short-term dynamics to take care of the respective economic cycles.

The long-term relationship compares the per capita GDP level of the previous period with the current level as explained by the fundamentals. The pace at which a potential gap between the two will shrink in the future is determined by country-specific convergence coefficients. This procedure has the great advantage that long-term growth in a specific country is not only based on that country's historical experience but also on the estimated average growth relationship across all countries. This is extremely helpful for our purposes as a forecast for a country should not only be based on its own development over time. Instead, it has to be based on a general long-term relationship between the changes in drivers and GDP growth across all countries.

For 21 OECD countries our estimates with annual data from 1970 to 1998 show a significant long-term relationship between the per capita GDP of the 15 to 64 age group and population growth, the investment ratio, human capital and openness. A time trend is not significant, which indicates that our model comprehensively explains technological change. The estimated pace of convergence is relatively high: in most countries, a gap between actual GDP and its fundamental long-term equilibrium is reduced by half within roughly three years. The country-specific short-term dynamics allow a respectable, average goodness of fit of 0.65.

Since the structure of the emerging markets differs significantly from the structure of the OECD economies we have estimated a second, separate model for 12 emerging markets. The coefficients are similar to those for the OECD economies, although the precision of the estimates is lower. The long-term impact of a change in openness seems to be smaller in poorer countries than in the OECD economies. However, openness has risen more strongly in the emerging markets. Unfortunately, no data on human capital is available for Russia, so we were unable to include it in our regression for the emerging markets. The average measure of the goodness of fit for the emerging markets is also a fairly high 0.65, though.

Forecasting the Drivers

The four drivers in our econometric model thus are population growth, the investment ratio, human capital and openness. For these four time series we need forecasts up until 2020 that can subsequently be fed into the econometric equation. We have developed a three-stage process to do this.

In the first stage (extrapolation) it is the past development alone that determines the future course of each time series. For all 34 countries three drivers were extrapolated with the help of the respective best, and in some cases non-linear, time series procedure. The exception is population growth, for which we use the United Nation's forecasts as our baseline.

The second stage (cross-check) factors are found in the additional information gained from the historic and future developments in the other countries. In some cases the extrapolation results in levels or changes in the time series that differ starkly from those of other countries in the past and the future. We have systematically corrected these paths with the help of information from levels and changes from the other countries in order to dampen extreme projections. This stage was only required for the investment ratio and human capital; the extrapolation of the openness measure produced no extreme developments for any country. We call the outcome of the first two stages 'the baseline forecast'.

The third stage (trend analysis) is by far the most complex and is the key element of the entire project. It is applied to all four drivers. This innovative stage is designed to increase the reliability of the forecasts and to help recognise and model structural breaks. In this stage we assessed a broad range of information that is not contained in the extrapolated baseline forecast or other growth models. Internal and external knowledge from trend and future research about the individual countries can thus be systematically incorporated into the forecast.

The Trend Analysis

In an ongoing process Deutsche Bank Research monitors more than 40 trends from five categories: 'The individual and society', 'Institutions and the political environment', 'Organizational forms and markets', 'Innovation and technology', and 'Natural resources'. For the global growth centres project we have selected 21 trends that are likely to be particularly significant for future economic growth. Further selection criteria were a good understanding of the fundamental causes and reasons for the trend; robust evidence for the existence of the trend; sufficient breadth of the trend; and relevance for the coming 15 years.

In order to reduce the complexity of the model we first assessed the reciprocal effects among all 21 trends with respect to strength and direction in a 21x21 cross-impact matrix. Based on this information we then combined the individual trends by means of a cluster analysis (average linkage method) into 6 consistent trend clusters that are illustrated on the map in figure 4.2. Trends within a cluster pull in the same direction relative to other clusters; trends in clusters that are far apart may impede each other. An important advantage of this approach is that information about the development of one trend can simultaneously supply information about the other trends in the same cluster.

With the aid of a multitude of indicators that supply information about both the level of change and the changes in the various trends, we have examined how fast these trend clusters have developed in the past 10 to 15 years in the 34 countries. Then, using these indicators and the country knowledge of DBR we have constructed a forecast about the likely speed of the trend clusters during the forecast period until 2020. The decisive impact on our growth forecasts stems from the changes in the speed of the trend clusters over time – their acceleration or deceleration. If a trend cluster develops just as quickly in the future as in the past, then it provides no additional information beyond the simple extrapolation in our baseline forecast.

If the speed changes, the drivers will also develop in different ways – and GDP growth will change. For a number of emerging markets we have also factored in additional structural breaks that have been identified by our country experts: Turkey's bid to join the EU and the increasing political stability in Brazil will have an impact that our trend clusters cannot fully reflect.

The next section provides a very brief introduction to the six trend clusters and to the relevance of the clusters for the four drivers of our model and thus for the model-based forecast.

Figure 4.2 DBR trend map

The Six Trend Clusters

The Opening of Work and Society

'The opening of work and society' trend cluster refers to the ongoing process in which the rigid structures inherent in labour markets and societies are being dismantled, flexibility is being increased and more people are being integrated into the economy. Career paths and working environments are becoming more flexible, so the practice of doing the same job for the same employer for one's whole working life is becoming less important, making lifelong learning more important and resulting in more frequent changes of job duties and employers. Women gain more importance in employment, because more women are working and they are assuming positions with greater responsibility. We regard the city as the most efficient location in the knowledge-based society, providing the infrastructure that enables career (apart from agriculture and the skilled trades) and family to be combined as urbanisation rises. The city is also the first port of call for the increasing number of labour migrants from other countries.

Countries in which the trend cluster will develop faster than in the past should – in our opinion – exhibit a lower population growth than those where the speed of the trend remains unchanged, since the opportunity cost of bringing up children (salary foregone) is rising. More flexible labour markets also allow a higher investment ratio, because higher labour input boosts the return on capital. We assume that the opening of work will also positively impact upon the development of human capital (including lifelong learning), as more and more people will be able to obtain greater returns on their education. Migration across national borders should help to foster open trading relations with foreign countries.

Enlarging the Scope of Life

The 'enlarging the scope of life' trend cluster consists of two trends that clearly belong together: ageing populations and the expansion of the healthcare sector. The healthcare sector encompasses both the treatment of acute ailments as well as preventive measures and expenditure on conditions for which there is sometimes no medical requirement such as cosmetic surgery. We regard the rapid pace of technological progress as the key driver of this trend.

An acceleration of the 'enlarging the scope of life' trend cluster gives a strong boost to population growth by raising life expectancy. To a large extent, this cluster has already been factored into the UN's population projection. However, the latter relies heavily on extrapolation and does not take structural breaks into account. We expect a slight positive impact from the acceleration of the trend cluster on investment because the healthcare sector is becoming increasingly capital intensive. Human capital and openness will also improve faster as education and training will become increasingly important as life expectancy rises and because older societies will possibly cooperate more closely with younger societies. A detailed analysis of this trend cluster can be found in Bergheim (2006).

The Conquest of the Smallest Structures

The trend cluster 'the conquest of the smallest structures' comprises two technological and two institutional trends. Biotechnology will, in our opinion, become a major growth area, while microtechnology and nanotechnology become important areas of innovation. In addition, work on and with ever smaller components will tend to be promoted in many regions by better institutions. Regional economic cooperation and integration will also move closer and facilitate research and development in these sectors. Knowledge and intellectual property from these and other sectors will increasingly be traded between companies and research institutions, nationally as well as internationally.

This trend cluster impacts positively on the investment ratio as research and production in the biotech- and nanosegments are relatively capital intensive. We believe the trend cluster will also have a positive impact on human capital and openness.

Global Networking in Business and Politics

The 'global networking in business and politics' cluster comprises five trends from the institutions and markets categories. More and more market participants are becoming globally active; they will enter new sectors and encounter fewer and fewer state regulations worldwide. This will provide them with more opportunities to escape the rigid structures in their home countries. The importance of transnational companies of all sizes will grow, as will the influence of global institutions such as the IMF, the WTO and non-governmental organizations such as Greenpeace. Knowledge-intensive services will gain importance and these services will increasingly be provided across borders. In order to facilitate this, national product, labour and capital markets will be deregulated.

The 'Global networking in business and politics' cluster has in our view a distinctly positive impact on human capital as education is necessary to participate in these trends. Openness also increases much faster in countries where these trends become more pronounced than in societies where the intensity of the trends remains unchanged. By contrast, the cluster has no impact on population growth and only a limited positive impact on the investment ratio, as deregulation barely alters relative factor prices.

Process Virtualisation in Networks

'Process virtualisation in networks' will become more and more important in the coming years. It will bring together more and more participants via increasingly efficient channels; organizational and market processes will increasingly operate in virtual space. This is occurring because electronic networking is improving and becoming more widespread, enabling the virtual operation of ever faster and more complex processes. The links between humans and machines will strengthen via more intelligent interfaces and will ensure that this complexity does not overwhelm us. For example, networked customer databases will change the competitive landscape in e-commerce, as outlined in Hofmann (2005).

We assume that the investment ratio will be positively impacted upon, not least because the required infrastructure has to be built. Human capital should improve more strongly, as education and training will be facilitated by the new channels as well as by experiencing increased market demand. Networking and virtualisation will also facilitate cross-border exchanges.

The Restriction of Growth

The 'restriction of growth' cluster comprises all those trends that tend to put a brake on growth. They often exacerbate one another and hinder some of the other trends or their positive impact on economic growth. The potential for social frictions arises when income differentials widen or ethnic and religious tensions intensify. The threat from international terrorism is growing and leading to higher spending on security. That ties up resources that could be deployed more productively elsewhere. Natural resources like fossil fuels, clean air and water are becoming increasingly scarce.

Fossil fuels are likely to become much more expensive during the forecast period. Therefore, sustainable and environmentally-oriented development will become increasingly important.

The rise in energy prices applies worldwide. However, the impact on economic growth will vary from country to country – depending on their level of energy efficiency and net energy import ratio. Therefore, we need to treat this trend and its impact on the GDP growth of individual countries differently from the other trends and link it directly to per capita economic growth.

The combination of the two other trends in this cluster (social frictions and terrorism) has been treated just like the other five clusters. Any acceleration in the trends 'potential for social frictions rises' and 'threats from international terrorism increase' negatively impacts population growth and investment ratios as these countries become less attractive for people and capital. These countries will also be less likely to open themselves up to foreign countries if the speed of the trend is to remain the same as in the past.

Trend-based Adjustment of the Baseline Forecasts

In order to quantify the impact of the change in the speed of a trend cluster on the four drivers we have developed standardized multipliers for all countries in order to calculate a reasonable add-on to the baseline forecast. What constitutes 'reasonable' is assessed relative to the average level of the drivers in 2002, as well as to their average increase in the past and their variance across countries. For example, we add 0.8 years of education in 2020 to a country where the speed of the trend cluster 'the opening of work and society' accelerates from 'high' to 'very high'. In the years preceding 2020 the add-on is applied on a pro rata basis. This approach allows only one structural break today and no further changes in speed during the forecast period.

In some emerging markets our country analysts expect significant structural breaks that are not factored into our general framework. The prospect of accession to the EU will reduce the hitherto high volatility of institutions and inflation rates in Turkey. For Brazil we also expect a structural break towards much more stable domestic institutions, the scale of which cannot be factored into our trend analysis. Therefore, the investment ratio and trade openness will rise much faster in both countries than if these structural breaks were not taken into account. Our country analysts also expect China to open up even more actively than assumed in our trend analysis: they expect the increase in openness during the last five years to continue at a similar pace.

The cumulative add-ons resulting from our analysis of the six trend clusters in the 34 countries can easily be recovered from the model. For example, human capital in Germany, Japan, India and China should improve by almost one year more than in the baseline forecast between 2005 and 2020. In Germany and Japan the main reasons are the expected acceleration of the trend clusters 'the opening of work and society' and 'process virtualisation in networks', whereas in India and China the

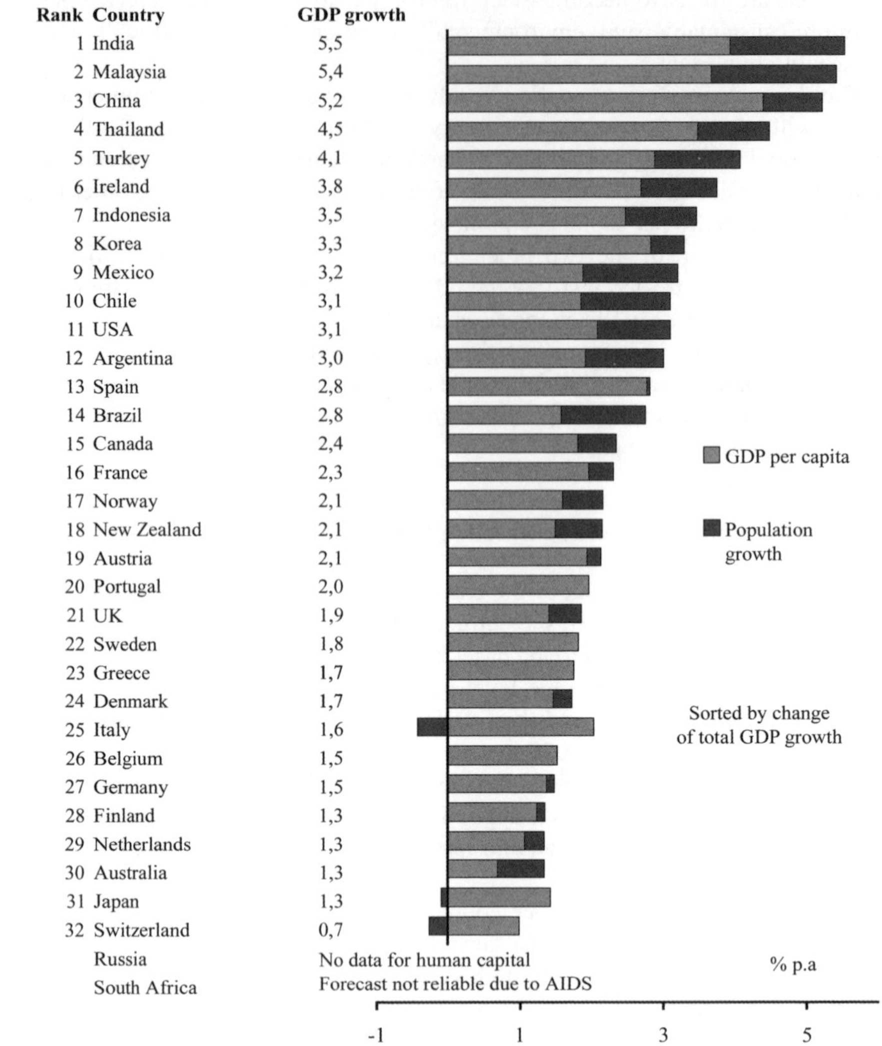

Figure 4.3 ***Formel-G*: ranking of GDP growth 2006-2020**

acceleration of 'global networking' is the main factor that will boost incentives for education.

At the final stage the forecasts for the four drivers are fed into the econometric model. This calculates annual growth rates for GDP per capita for the 15 to 64 age group until 2020. Using our own population forecasts for both this group and the population as a whole enables the calculation of the levels and growth rates of GDP overall and GDP per capita.

Results: The Growth Stars of 2006–2020

The star in our global growth ranking is India, with an expected annual average rate of GDP growth of 5.5 per cent over the years 2006 to 2020. This model forecast is roughly in line with the current consensus expectations. With a growth rate of 5.5 per cent, real GDP doubles every 13 years. As a result, India will – in purchasing power parity (PPP) terms – take the place of Japan as the world's third-largest economy behind the US and China by the end of this decade. A strong population growth of 1.6 per cent per annum from 2006 to 2020 will contribute significantly to overall GDP growth. But per capita GDP is also set to rise significantly, by 3.9 per cent, as human capital will improve rapidly and India will probably continue to open strongly to the rest of the world. With that growth rate, per capita GDP growth doubles every 18 years. However, per capita income in India will still be the second lowest in our group of countries by 2020. Compared to Germany, India's per capita income will rise from 10 per cent today to 16 per cent. In mid-2005, Deutsche Bank Research launched a new 'megatopic' covering India in more depth. The other introductory study that also provides scenarios and sector analysis is Asuncion-Mund (2005).

Malaysia's economy of 25 million inhabitants is set to continue the success of the last two decades. According to the *Formel-G*, Malaysia's average annual GDP growth is projected to be 5.4 per cent from 2006 to 2020 – almost as high as in much poorer India. At 3.6 per cent, the rise in per capita GDP would match the growth rate of 1976 to 2000. By 2020 Malaysia's economy will probably be larger than Belgium's or Sweden's (in purchasing power parities). In a few years' time, its per capita income level in PPPs will be higher than Chile's or Mexico's.

China comes in at third place in our overall growth ranking, with a projected annual GDP growth of 5.2 per cent over the years 2006 to 2020. At that rate, China will not become the largest economy of the world by 2020. Growth will be even stronger at the beginning of the forecast period with rates of initially almost 7 per cent – albeit below the medium-term consensus forecast of 8 per cent and the average rate of 10 per cent of the past two decades. The model enables us to explain why China will be overtaken by India. The growth differential between China and India stems only from the much slower population growth of China (0.8 per cent per year). This is the effect of two decades of the one-child-policy, which will become evident in the growth diffrential. The projected average per capita income of the Chinese will rise by 4.4 per cent annually, topping the rate of increase in India. By 2020 China's per capita income in purchasing power parities is set to surpass that of Brazil and almost match Turkey's level.

Latin American countries rank at the bottom end of the growth league among the emerging markets. Mexico's proximity to the US and open trade with the US market, will enable it to be just ahead of Argentina and Brazil. In all three countries the drivers of growth are rather weak even though per capita growth rates are set to improve when compared to the past. Mexico's path into 2020 is analysed in detail in Voss (2006).

A lack of data prevents us from fully including Russia in our framework. However, a noticeably shrinking population and high political uncertainty do not bode well for overall GDP growth going forward. DBR's country experts put Russia's growth potential in the coming years at roughly 4 per cent – slower thereafter. Growth will be partly driven by the expected increase in energy prices, which should benefit Russia as a major exporter of oil and gas.

Growth rates are not everything. Current per capita income levels are also of major importance for the attractiveness of a country as a location especially for exports of up-market products. Furthermore, the closest trade and FDI links today are found among the rich economies. We have therefore produced a separate ranking for the rich countries.

Formel-G projects a 3.8 per cent average annual GDP growth in Ireland from 2006 to 2020, so it is set to remain the top performer among the rich countries. The forecast of 1.1 per cent population growth per annum is the highest among the richer economies. GDP per capita will rise by almost 3 per cent per year. However, a large share of the income generated in Ireland goes to foreigners, so the income of the average Irish is lower than the comparison of GDP levels would suggest. With a population of just 4.7 million in 2020, Ireland will have the second-lowest population in our group and is thus not too significant as a sales market.

The USA shows that even economies with high income levels can achieve high growth rates of per capita GDP. With GDP growth expected to reach 3 per cent per year, the US ranks second among the rich countries, mainly because it remains at the forefront of technological progress. Thanks to population growth of 1 per cent and per capita GDP growth of 2 per cent, the US economy will continue to post the highest level of GDP overall and per capita in 2020.

Spain's fundamentals, such as the expected strong rises in human capital and trade openness (as a bridge between Europe and Latin America and North Africa), also point to solid growth ahead: with annual per capita GDP growth expected to run at 2.8 per cent Spain surpasses all other European countries. If immigration continues at the same pace as in the last few years, overall growth could be even higher: the UN population forecasts included in our model have underestimated actual population growth by a full percentage point during recent years since immigration from North Africa and Latin America has more than compensated for the low birth rate.

In addition to Spain, France and Austria are set to post the strongest economic expansion in Europe according to our growth ranking. This is attributable to solid population growth and strong fundamentals. In Italy a sharp rise in human capital will contribute to strong per capita GDP growth. With a growth rate of 1.5 per cent, Germany ranks at the lower end of the league table, while Switzerland is at the bottom with 0.7 per cent.

The Limits of *Formel–G*

Transparency is one of the advantages of *Formel-G*: For each country we can analyse the main contributors to growth and the country-specific strengths and weaknesses. The sound theoretical underpinnings, the new empirical methods, the extensive cross-country comparisons and above all the innovative trend analyses are the other strengths of this long-term model.

However, the model also has limits and shortcomings. First of all, there are the usual uncertainties of every forecasting model: the slope coefficients in the econometric equation (for example the structure of the economies) could be different in the future than in the past; the restriction of the same long-run coefficients could be inappropriate for some countries; and the assumptions regarding the trend clusters might prove to be incorrect. In addition, many emerging markets have a volatile past consisting of many exceptional situations. This reduces the reliability of forecasts for South Africa and Turkey, for example. Dramatic events, such as a reunification of the two Koreas, uprisings against authoritarian governments or military conflict with neighbouring countries cannot be predicted by our model. They need to be handled with separate scenario analyses.

In the long-term equilibrium analysed here, interest rates, exchange rates, government deficits and current account balances do not play a role – they are neutral. If a country pursues a short-term expansionary business cycle policy that pushes GDP above its fundamental equilibrium, the model then forecasts a convergence back towards this equilibrium. However, it cannot forecast how long these variables remain away from their neutral levels. However, in the long term, an expansionary business cycle policy does not help. As mentioned above, a fundamentally unjustifiable gap to the fundamentals is reduced by half within three years.

The model possibly also has problems with fully taking into account an increase in the employment rate caused by, for example, an increase in the retirement age. We factor in this possibility via the trend cluster the 'the opening of work and society' which explains among other things the high trend mark-up for Germany.

The model does not factor the impact of externalities that lead to a trend in the concentration of economic activity. These externalities are responsible for some regional divergence for example within Germany and the US. Another example is that economic activity in Asia may be concentrated around Shanghai – which would mean that countries further away from Shanghai could actually do worse than is forecast by the model.

Chapter 5

A Political Early Warning-response System to Address Global and Regional Threats

Tapio Kanninen

Introduction

In this essay I discuss how the international community could conceptualise, understand and react to global and regional threats. The recent United Nations' (UN) High-level Panel on Threats, Challenges and Change, and other world commissions, have outlined the increased threats to humanity in the 21st century, as also discussed briefly in this article. In relation to that I first present a simple framework to assess the trends of the future with illustrative examples of its application. Secondly, I discuss how this framework could be more systematic, or quantified, based on the history of similar efforts in economic, social, environmental and political fields. Finally, I present a tentative global response system, based on the framework, to react to emerging threats to the international community in the years and decades to come.

Conceptual Framework

We usually approach the future in an intuitive way. Our implicit mental models are not made explicit and we tend to change the variables of this perceptional lens from time to time. The results of an ever-moving mental environment better support – we tend to think unconsciously – our secret agendas, political preferences, hidden or pronounced values and moods of the day. If this is part and parcel of the art and science of the future it reduces its credibility and claim to be taken seriously in the field of research and analysis.

I believe we should reduce this haphazardness by making explicit the inherent assumptions, variables and relations we use. I am proposing here a generic conceptual framework of analysis for assessing future trends, globally and regionally. An overall framework could help us to formulate our questions about the future in a more credible and comprehensive way than before. Furthermore, a relatively simple framework as proposed here could assist in reducing the complexity of the future to manageable means.

First, let us take a look at the figure below. Its major parameters and relations could help us to better understand the forces shaping the future:

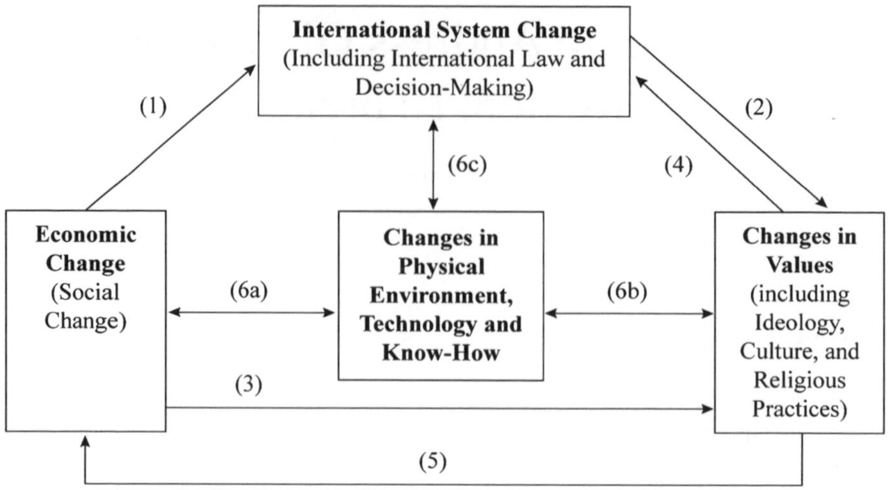

Figure 5.1 A simple framework to analyse the future: relations between economic, systemic, environmental and ideological change

In order to discuss the future we have to be speculative. It is best to do this in an economic and transparent way, and thus a more credible and useful way for most people, by applying only a relatively few key concepts and relationships. If we can play only with a limited number of categories this increases the usefulness of the framework as everyone can use it, experiment with it and test it in practice. An overly complicated model tends to confuse rather than illuminate.[1]

A central argument here is that the parameters and relations described in figure 5.1 – economic change in key countries and regions; ideological change in the international community; international systemic change; and change in physical environments including advances in communications, educational systems and technology – provide a useful evaluation framework for assessing the future. It should be powerful enough to explain major trends and their expected interactions:

1 The original version of this model was presented in my 1990 Ph.D. dissertation *Leadership and Reform: The Secretary-General and the UN Financial Crisis of the late 1980s*, published by Kluwer Law International in 1995, The Hague, pp. 252 – 253. In order to explain the repeated financial crises of the World Organization, and predict them in the future, I created a comprehensive model of all the variables and relations affecting the financial situation of the UN. The only new variables in the model in this essay are the changes in physical environment, technology and know-how.

what has happened during previous decades, what is happening at the moment and what will happen if such trends are described in broad terms.

Key questions in using the framework are: what are the units of its application, what is the level of analysis and what are the actors involved: a state, a regional or intergovernmental agency, an international or non-governmental organization, a corporation, a network? The framework is meant to be all-encompassing, and still heuristic – and thus useful for creating a global early warning-response system as later explained in this essay. To specify the level of analysis or a specific actor is not necessary at this broad conceptual level. Rather, it is the combined effect of all actors which makes the biggest difference. Of course, when the framework is used for a given purpose actors should be identified. In the examples that follow the country level is mostly used as a unit of analysis. As many futurologists see a network emerging as a more powerful unit of analysis than a nation-state, the framework could easily be adopted for network-based scenarios as necessary.

The framework is not a theory in a strict scientific sense of the word but a pre-theory, a conceptual model. As shown later in the paper this is enough for our purpose, based on historical evidence, to create a new response system for monitoring and responding to global and regional threats. In the longer run, however, a more sophisticated theory for global monitoring and reaction could be developed.

Examples of the Use of the Conceptual Framework

The section that follows gives examples of some tentative assumptions about the future based on this framework. It then describes factual situations in the world of yesterday, today and its future by outlining some of the major global and regional threats associated with interactions between the variables of the framework. The test of the usefulness of the framework is:

1. Whether it helps in understanding world problems in a comprehensive, interrelated manner;

2. Whether it leads us to think about the key variables and their relations, or chain reactions, in a way which we would not be intuitively inclined to do;

3. Whether it could be used as a checklist of the most pertinent variables and their relations in order to make a reliable analysis of future trends; and

4. Whether it could provide a useful agenda for the global and regional monitoring of trends, threats and their required responses by decision-makers.

I use selected examples to illustrate the use of the framework. Many of them are taken from the report of the High-level Panel on Threats, Challenges and Change Secretary-General Kofi Annan established in 2003 (UN 2004). These 16 wise men and women, and its research secretariat, represent the thinking of the United Nations about the future challenges facing the world at the start of the 21st century. Many of its findings were reiterated in the Secretary-General's own report *In Larger Freedom*

(Annan 2005) and many, but not all, were included subsequently by the heads of State and Governments at the 2005 World Summit Outcome document approved in September 2005 (UN General Assembly 2005b).

Another person might describe the facts inside each box and along each arrow in figure 5.1 differently than is done here. The point is not to make a case through the power of facts but rather to illustrate the usefulness of the framework. Variations between the facts while still using the same framework will provide another useful analysis. A case made in the last section of this essay is that we need a relatively simple conceptual framework in order to create a systematic early warning-response system for global monitoring. Better data will follow automatically – if history is our guide – when a proper framework is first created. But a long term goal should indeed be the creation of a more standardized framework at the international level for global reporting that will ultimately make the collection of the data more systematic and reliable, as explained in more detail later.

The future direction of the relations of the boxes in figure 5.1, linked by the arrows, is argued to be developing along the following lines:

Arrow 1, Economic Change[2] in Relation to International Systemic Change. Will Emerging Economic Powerhouses and Regions Press for a Larger Role in the World's Political Decision-making?

The Hypothetical Assumption of Trends

Paul Kennedy (1987), among others, has provided arguments on the predominance of the economic base in determining the relative power of nations in the world system. Those great powers that overstretch their reach and dominance will eventually shrink. The changes taking place in national and regional economies will gradually affect the whole international system[3] and, over time, the global international system will evolve to reflect the multipolar character of world relations and their economic base. Multipolarity and economic interconnectedness also mean more complex international relations in which no major actor can totally dominate the world political scene. Regional actors might, through economic integration, also strengthen their roles in the world system.

Are the changes in national economic variables increasing the political power of

2 Social change, such as caused by migration or the dramatic outbreak of infectious diseases, is an additional layer in this box. It will affect economic change directly, and vice versa, but also have an impact on other variables in the framework. It is not taken, however, as an independent variable because we wish to keep the framework simple. Another assumption is that economic change is a more powerful variable than social change in explaining future trends. But if reality proves otherwise the framework could be changed accordingly. Theoretically, international economic, financial and trade laws, standards and regulations also affect economic development (a feedback loop from international systemic change to economic change) but these relations are not considered the most important ones in understanding the future and are not discussed here.

3 The international system refers here to the international order that was first created by the League of Nations and then more conclusively in San Francisco in 1945.

some countries and regions in the international system in today's world when using the nation-state as a unit of analysis? Are we moving away from political unipolarity to multipolarity and increased multilateralism based on the economic performance of the superpowers of the future?

The Exploration of Facts

A good example of the evolving relationship of the two variables – economic vs. political – is the strengthened relative economic power of Japan and Germany and how this new role is reflected in the past, present and future international system. Both countries have been convinced since the early 1990s that their economic world power has increased to the level which should entitle them a permanent seat in the UN Security Council. However, the Council is not an economic institution but the most influential political body in the world according to international law and the UN Charter. Economic power has to be recognized in the political system of the world, Japan and Germany seem to argue.

In fall 2004 and spring 2005 Japan and Germany teamed up with Brazil and India – rising economic and political powerhouses in the developing world – to make a joint effort to propose a package deal before the World Summit in September 2005 in the aftermath of the proposals of the Secretary-General's High-level Panel (UN General Assembly 2005a). The High-level Panel had suggested that Security Council decision-making should be reformed so that the representations of those that 'contribute' most to the United Nations should be substantially increased. Japan has been for a long time a top contributor to the UN regular budget – 19.5 per cent – after the U.S., 22 per cent, and Germany at 8.7 per cent close to the top. From the permanent members Russia pays only 1.1 per cent and China 2.1 per cent and the shares of the U.K. (6.1 per cent) and France (6.0 per cent) are below Japan's and Germany's percentages (UN Secretariat 2005)

The efforts of 'the Group of Four' – as they were called – failed in summer 2005 but similar efforts will most likely be tried in the future. Most analysts think that it was not the U.S. who blocked the reform but the Africans who could not agree on joint candidates for the permanent members from their continent. The Group of Four – which suggested two permanent members for Africa – needed their votes for the reform in the General Assembly. As enough votes for the proposal were not assured, the effort was not pursued to the end in 2005. A new struggle might still lie ahead as some Japanese Parliamentarians have threatened to cut the country's funding to the UN and there is considerable uneasiness among the Japanese that they contribute much to the UN budget without adequate political representation.

Another example of the economic-political nexus is China's rising economic power which has brought about a clear increase in its political influence in world affairs. The U.S. has recently made major political efforts to contain and modify China's influence in Asia (Perez 2006). China and other Asian states have been the bankers of the U.S. trade deficit which makes the U.S. and China more interdependent economically, as well as politically. The potential vulnerability of new global-regional financial arrangements between American and Asian economies could be a major threat for future financial relations within the world, affected as much by political as well as financial considerations. (*A Grand Strategy to Reinvigorate US Leadership* 2005)[4].

The increased multipolarity in the world system is demonstrated by the fact that, although the U.S. has maintained its military superiority the other economic centres in the world – China, Japan and the EU in particular – have forced the U.S. to take into account the wishes of other major global economic players. In the 2005 reform effort of the Security Council, although the U.S. was less than enthusiastic about the reform in general – as an enlarged Council will reduce or at least complicate its major influence in the body – it had to back Japan's bid for the reform. Earlier the U.S. had been a supporter of Germany's permanent membership as well but Germany's initial stand on the Iraq war caused at least a temporary suspension of American support.

Italy has opposed the permanent membership of Germany and many Asian countries have been reluctant to give such a membership to Japan. A proposal to create a joint European permanent seat for the EU, as a compromise, has been opposed by France and the U.K. But a more democratic and regionally representative Council might be one of the trends in future reform efforts, an issue we return to later in this essay.

Regionalism was a major trend at the San Francisco Conference in 1945 in order to oppose globalism or universalism, which was seen as a less 'democratic' approach to international affairs as it granted veto powers to the Security Council for the winners of the Second World War. (Graham and Felicio 2006, Schlesinger 2003)[5]. There are signs of its gradual re-emergence as a major factor in the international system based on the economic integration of regions and subregions. A number of previously solely economic unions such as the EU, the Inter-Governmental Authority on Development (IGAD) and the Economic Community of West African States (ECOWAS) have transformed into political organs exerting influence both in the regions and – in the case of the EU in particular – in the world.

Arrow 2, International Systemic Change in Relation to Ideological Change. Increased Economic Multipolarity Requires Better Coordination but Multilateral Measures Have to Bring about Credible Results: Will the UN's and the Regional Agencies' Ideologies Change Accordingly?

The Hypothetical Assumption of Trends

As political and economic factors are more intertwined than before – partly as a result of multipolarity and economic interconnectedness – they provide new breeding grounds for conflicts. The end of the Cold War meant the re-emergence of many regional conflicts as the only remaining superpower was unwilling or unable to create Cold War types of constraints for local disputes. Regional threats increasingly

4 'In 2005 Stanley Foundation Strategy for Peace Conference, noting the extraordinary degree of US interdependence with China, a participant said the two were locked into "mutually assured depression" ' (A Grand Strategy to Reinvigorate US Leadership 2005).

5 On monitoring regional integration, see <www.cris.unu.edu>.

require preventive and management efforts by actors other than the big powers. These new managers might be emerging economic powers, middle powers, regional agents and international organizations, or influential non-governmental organizations like the Carter Centre, former Finnish President Martti Ahtisaari's Conflict Management Initiative (CMI) and the Community of Sant'Egidio. The existing superpower, the U.S., no longer has such a unilateral, bilateral or multilateral leverage as before. The UN, on the other hand, has come under pressure to do more and do it more effectively.

At the same time, as the ideological and cultural climate in the world changes as a result of systemic change, it puts more stress on multilateralism and on related values in order to respond to increased global multipolarity.[6] Values will gradually change accommodating the need for better international coordination and crisis management. This puts even more pressure on UN management reforms. Regional organizations, such as the AU and OAS, and intergovernmental organizations, such as NATO, have to deliver better results as well.

The Exploration of Facts

The UN could be seen as one of the key managers of the international system although by far not the only one. Its political activities and scope of assistance to member states have clearly increased over the years. Any new values and ideological changes in the world will also affect the leadership and management of the World Organization.

The recent criticism of the management of the United Nations – coming mostly but not exclusively from the Americans – could be seen in this light.[7] As a result of a gradual relative power change in the international system the U.S. needs more than ever before the UN as a global or regional manager of conflicts and other problems that the U.S. does not want to handle, as well as on occasion, to legitimize its actions. But if the UN is given more important tasks it has to be more efficient, transparent

6 Values and culture are related: values create a pattern of behaviour in a society which could be called a specific 'culture' in that society. A pattern of coherent values forms an ideology. Values in this essay are deeply-held beliefs and normative standards for behaviour.

7 One of the strongest criticisms comes from Claudia Rosett, a journalist in residence with the Foundation for the Defense of Democracies. She says: 'Now the UN, in contravention of its own charter, is rapidly evolving into something larger, more corporate, and more menacing: a predatory, undemocratic, unaccountable, and self-serving vehicle for global government... Unwieldy, gross, inefficient, and incompetent...' (Rosett 2006). For some critics, whatever the UN has done or will do is probably analysed from this perspective. This criticism could be seen as an illustration that the UN has become politically more important and, on the other hand, also a creator of economic activity of tens of billions of dollars. As the UN has been given more tasks, its expanded reach provides more employment for its staff, consultants, vendors and other businesses benefiting directly or indirectly from the UN activities, as well as creating more jobs for its proponents (like the staff of national UN Associations all over the world) and some, although still very few, for its critics. The larger the organization is, the more opportunities it also provides for corruption and mismanagement.

and accountable; it has to be a more credible conflict and world issues manager than before.

But it is not only the U.S. that requests changes in the UN´s management. The whole international community needs a new and better UN as the number of threats to international peace and security are more severe than ever before and have became manifold. Whoever the key managers of regional threats and world problems are, they should be internally managed more effectively, more competently. The High-level Panel reflected upon this challenge and identified the following threats (UN High-level Panel on Threats, Challenges and Change 2004):

1. Economic and social threats, including poverty, infectious disease and environmental degradation;
2. Inter-state conflict;
3. Internal conflict, including civil war, genocide and other large-scale atrocities;
4. Nuclear, radiological, chemical and biological weapons;
5. Terrorism; and
6. Transnational organized crime.

These are no small challenges and the Panel concluded that the UN has to reform itself to be able to tackle the threats. These issues were the subject of major debates at the 2005 World Summit. One ensuing response, as far the UN was concerned, was Kofi Annan's management reform proposal in March 2006 (Annan 2006). On the other hand, the UN reforms are continuous, periodic re-emerging exercises that follow similar patterns with some variations, patterns that are found in all large public organizations and even in the private sector (Kanninen 1990).

The world leaders also declared that regional organizations should be strengthened and that a better distribution of labour with the UN has to be found. The UN cannot do everything alone in conflict prevention, resolution, peace-keeping and peace-building. During the last decade, the heads of regional and other intergovernmental organizations have indeed intensified their internal cooperation with the United Nations, and decided in 2005 to meet henceforth annually under the chairmanship of the UN Secretary-General instead of the previous biennial cycle.

In changing times, even the key concepts receive new interpretations in order to be able to provide new mandates for organizational requirements aimed at better addressing global and regional threats.

In finding answers to emerging challenges the High-level Panel provided a new interpretation of collective security. In earlier decades, collective security was only seen in military terms. Now – reflecting the new values of the last decades – the Panel first declared that, in order to be credible, collective security should be 'effective, efficient and equitable'. Following Secretary-General Kofi Annan's 2001 report on the prevention of armed conflict the Panel also recognized that prevention is an indispensable foundation of collective security. The Secretary-General had suggested in his 2001 report that 'conflict prevention be the cornerstone of the collective security system of the UN in the 21st century' (Annan 2001). The prevention concept – whether used in the avoidance of an armed conflict, an ecological disaster or a terrorist attack – is becoming a new multidimensional framework, an overarching concept, a new multilateral religion in the management of world affairs in the 21st century (Kanninen 2003).

The prevention of conflicts and global and regional threats, a fundamental concept already in Article 1 of the UN Charter, might therefore become a re-born ideology of the United Nations. But also regional organizations have placed conflict prevention higher on their priority lists for action. A UNU survey found that prevention was the most unifying common area of interest for all organizations reviewed (Graham, Felicio and Tavares 2006). But other values will also affect the emerging and turbulent international scene, as we see in the next section.

Arrow 3, Economic Change in Relation to Ideological Change. Question 1: Will the Economic Winners Make an Imprint on Global Values?

The successful economic performance of emerging powerhouses and regions will make an imprint on the business values of other countries and regions reinforcing the values of the management culture of the economic winners. Assuming the continuous economic success of Asian countries these values might be, based on a poll taken in seven Asian countries: *Personal Values*: hard work; respect for learning; honesty; self-discipline; self-reliance – and *Top Societal Values*: an orderly society; harmony; the accountability of public officials; openness to new ideas; freedom of expression; and respect for authority. (Hitchcock 1997).

On the other hand, the promotion of democracy, human rights and other freedoms – another ongoing trend – have been seen as Western values, not necessary or applicable, for instance, to Asian and Arab traditions. But democracy is spreading as a value around the world – at an increasing pace – and two world-wide movements on democracy have spearheaded, with some success, its broader acceptance in new countries and regions. The older movement, the Conference of New or Restored Democracies, started indeed in Asia, in the Philippines in 1988 with 13 countries participating. Its 6th International Conference is scheduled to take place in Doha, Qatar, in October 2006, for the first time in the Arab region, with far over 100 countries expected to attend. Another movement, the Community of Democracies, initiated and sponsored most consistently by the United States, started in Poland in 2000 and has its 4th International Conference scheduled to take place in Mali in 2007. The first movement is open-ended; the latter is a group with a limited membership selected by a small 'convening group' of counties. (Dumitriu 2005).

But how would the application of Asian values tested mostly in business practice coincide with the principles of democracy? Not many Asian countries have used democracy widely in the past, or at least not a Western model. But countries in Asia are following the world trend. China, for instance, issued its first White Paper on democracy in October 2005 emphasizing 'socialist democracy with Chinese characteristics' and the importance of the Communist Party in remaining in charge of the process.[8]

If Asian values are used more widely, would all components of democracy be applied or only a selected few? For instance, would the globally felt pressure for increased transparency and the accountability of large public organizations, including financial and economic organizations, mean that they all would be required to increase their auditing and inspection practices? The UN has recently gone through an expanding number of internal and external inquiries, as have many large private companies in the U.S., as the outrage of corruption has become a priority concern and a value of its own. Would the next inspection wave hit the Bretton Woods organizations, the WTO and the world's other financial and commercial institutions as priorities might change and require closer audits of major multilateral economic actors as well?

Arrow 3, Economic Change in Relation to Ideological Change. Question 2: Will Globalization Values Clash with Those of Democratization?

Privatisation, deregulation, and increased competition, the prominent economic values since the 1980s, have been applied increasingly in the world scene. The world´s management culture has changed accordingly. The acceleration of globalization has been one result of the application of these values. The continuous application of privatisation, trade and market liberalization and deregulation principles will, however, require more attention be paid to the harmonization aspects of national, corporate and individual actions at global and regional levels as well as the continuous monitoring of potential cases of corruption and conflict of interest.[9]

But there are also severe ethical and social implications with regard to globalization, the result of the continuous use of business values over the last decades: increasing gaps between haves and have-nots within and between countries and regions.[10] Some say that globalization has not markedly changed existing inequalities but has changed the expectations of the have-nots to be more equal with others. On the other hand, the concept of democracy – a value spreading across regions through globalization – stresses the equality of all individuals. Therefore, will there be an emerging new clash between globalization and democratization and how could the

8 <http://www.china.org.cn/english/2005/Oct/145718.htm>

9 Some changes are already taking place. In order to harmonize business ethics to make them better fit the accepted standards of the international community, Secretary-General Kofi Annan announced in Davos in 1999 the creation of the Global Compact. It is a consistent effort to enlist corporations in the world and get them to embrace, support and enact a set of core values in the areas of human rights, labour standards, the environment and anti-corruption. The UN has also paid more attention to the accountability and transparency of its staff. Kofi Annan recently established an independent Ethics Office as part of his management reform.

10 Data may vary on the impact of globalization. 'The problem is that the statistics describe the different stories depending on the methodology one prefers', (Naim 2006). This observation supports the point made in this essay that there is a considerable need to create a systematic and internationally acceptable framework for monitoring global and regional trends.

values of globalization and democracy better coincide? These are major challenges for the international community in the years to come.

What are the linkages between globalization and democratization? Promoting democracy and free markets are often seen as related undertakings. John Naisbitt, for instance, saw democracy as a 'free-market democracy' increasing through globalization (Naisbitt 1995). Jagdish Bhagwati says that globalization promotes democracy while constraining it (Bhagwati 2004). Taking a contrary view to democracy optimism, Heikki Patomaki thinks that democracy is drastically decreasing in countries because the democratic space of decision-making has decreased due to globalization. Similarly, the eminent researchers of the American Political Science Association warned that wide and growing socio-economic inequalities in the U.S. are undermining its practices and the procedures of liberal-democracy (Patomaki 2005).

The use of the values of the two major clusters of recent modernization trends, globalization and democratization, might have opposite effects – at least in the way they are applied today. Globalization has increased technical opportunities for practicing democracy in an increasing number of countries and regions but has not correspondingly increased economic opportunities for all, restricting the space for the use of democracy. Elections are just a small part of democracy. Inequalities or expectations to be more equal have increased in countries and between countries and regions, with Africa being left far behind other regions.[11] Is it possible that the legitimacy of democracy could decline if this clash in the use and impacts of 'economic values' (privatisations, deregularisation, liberalisation) and 'political values' (freer and wider participation in elections and all decision-making affecting an individual) is not bridged?

In seeking answers to these problems we have to examine the feedback loop in arrow 4, the impact of 'ideological change' on 'international system change', an issue to which we now turn.

Arrow 4, Feedback Loop. Ideological Change in Relation to International Systemic Change. Will Globalization and Its Effects on Inequality Bring Pressure to Increase Global and Regional Democracy?

Increased multipolarity, complexity and multilateralism combined with the application of efficiency, deregulation and privatisation principles will bring about more pressures for enhanced coordination and the harmonisation of the international system, including its economic and financial base. The negative effects of globalization have to be managed and rectified.

We already discussed the overall linkages between globalization and democratization but more specifically, what is globalization's impact on democracy? Joseph Stiglitz says that because globalization has been mismanaged millions have not enjoyed its benefits and millions have even been made worse off. He uses the term 'democratic globalization' which means that the decisions on globalization must be made with the full participation of all the peoples of the world. 'Our system of global

11 See footnote 10.

governance without global government can only work if there is an acceptance of multilateralism,' he says. (Stiglitz 2003). Would this mean that major decisions on globalization should be made in the future more democratically than at present?

The Exploration of Facts

As far as the UN is concerned there have been repeated calls to democratize the Organization. Regional and country representation, plus the veto powers of the permanent members of the Security Council are not democratic in the usual meaning of the word. The decision-making structures of the Bretton Woods institutions are not democratic either. Following this line of argumentation, Secretary-General Boutros Boutros-Ghali (1996) wanted to extend democratization from traditional democracy promotion in countries to regional and international democratization. The Movement of Non-Aligned Countries (NAM), a group of 116 countries, has for its part promoted a version of global democracy as it has spoken for a more democratic UN and Security Council, including the elimination of the veto powers of the permanent five on the Council.[12] Civil society has also been demanding more global democracy for some time. A Network Institute for Global Democratization, established in 1997, was created solely for this purpose.[13]

Another aspect of globalization has been its impact on cultures and civilizations. Globalization has provided the technological means for all countries, cultures, religions and ideologies of the world to be in constant communication. If, however, values, lifestyles and economic benefits clash there has to be an effort to promote intercultural and inter-civilizational tolerance and dialogue. This goal should also lead to a search to find ways and means to bridge the gap between Arab, Asian, African and Western forms of democracy, as necessary, or at least to understand better the differences between various models of democracy.

The UN announced 2001 as the year of the dialogue of civilizations and developed a programme of action to promote such a dialogue. The most recent effort is an Alliance of Civilizations initiative, a high-level panel spearheaded by Spain and Turkey. The initiative will give its report to the Secretary-General, with recommendations for future measures, at the end of 2006. The UN has therefore already become a forum for discussing the 'clashes, dialogues and alliances of civilizations'. The next logical step would be a discussion on 'clashes between globalization and democratization'. This trend of expanding the agenda of democratization and globalization's effects on democracy was already seen in the discussions of the Ulaanbaatar Conference of New or Restored Democracies in 2003.

In order to alleviate the impact of globalization's negative aspects there might be a need to increase the space of democracy, globally, regionally and nationally. Would this mean that we need discussion on how democratic values could be used in decision-making that is truly at the centre of globalization: in the Bretton Woods institutions,

12 The Cartagena Summit of October 1995 declared that the veto power was contrary to the aim of the democratization of the UN and must therefore be curtailed with a view to its elimination. See <www.globalpolicy.org/security/reform/egypt.htm>.

13 See <www.nigd.org>

the WTO as well as the multilateral corporations that are in fact much bigger than many UN member states? Joseph Stiglitz (2003) expresses this unresolved concern in the following way: 'Part of the problem lies with the international economic institutions, with the IMF, World Bank, and WTO, which help set the rules of the game. They have done so in ways that, all too often, have served the interests of the more advanced industrial countries – and particular interests within those countries – rather than those of the developing world'.

The demand for democracy has both global and regional aspects: In terms of regional democracy the Seoul Plan of Action adopted at the 2nd Community of Democracy Conference in the Republic of Korea in 2002 and the Ulaanbaatar Plan of Action, adopted at the 5th International Conference of New or Restored Democracies in Mongolia in 2003, set up ambitious plans for deepening democracy in the regions. Regional plans for democracy will be discussed at the next International Conference of New or Restored Democracies in Doha in October 2006. Two Asian countries and an Arab country have been, or will be, at the centre of the international discussion on deepening democracy in the world, a sign of changing times.

The movement of New or Restored Democracies has also broadened the scope of its participants beyond governments and its periodic conferences now include separate forums for civil society and parliamentarians. Whether regional organizations should also have a separate forum of their own is a question for the future: Boutros Boutros-Ghali (1996, 23) expressed his view on their role in the international system in the following way: 'The integration of regional organizations into the United Nations system is a cornerstone of democratization internationally'.

Arrows 5 and 6 are not discussed here in detail as they would require much longer explanations. Some illustrative examples and questions are only meant to give some broad outlines of the relationships involved.

Arrow 5, Ideological Change's Feedback Loop to Economic Change. Will There Be a Backlash Against Globalization and the Promotion of Democracy Based on Their Unequal Economic Impact?

The promotion of democracy by major powers, the UN and regional agencies might in some regions increase economic growth but in other regions the linkage might be more problematic. Initiatives such as the American 'Greater Middle East Initiative' to promote democracy in the Arab world also have economic impacts. Political and military actions have recently made elections possible in the new political landscape of the Arab world, for instance, in Iraq and Palestine. At the same time the democratization process has had a major regional economic impact in terms of reconstruction, the price of oil or changing patterns of foreign assistance. Would one type of democracy or another fit well in the culture and traditions of the Middle East and how quick could the pace of democratization be? Should the proposals for more democracy come only from the region? Would rapid democratization bring political and economic instability or stability in the area where conducting elections – without broader societal acceptance of the new values – might have an additional impact on the world economy, especially, when one is dealing with a region containing the most proven oil resources of the world?

More generally, the use of globalization principles and free-market democracy has given cause to anti-globalization movements as globalization has brought greater inequality or higher expectations for equality, to many parts of the world. The nationalisation of energy industries, as happened in Bolivia in May 2006, might be a sign of a new anti-trend within some Governments that have recently come to power. The rise of international militant fundamentalism and global terrorist movements, with their new deadly ideologies, also has had and will have a direct impact on economic development. For instance, the terrorist actions of the 11th of September 2001 have had a major economic world-wide impact. If the potential clashes of civilizations and those between globalization and democratization are not alleviated the failure might have a major impact on the world economy as well.

Arrow 6 (a), The Impact of Changes in the Physical Environment and Technology on Economic Change and Vice Versa. Will the Debates on the Limits to Growth Re-emerge?

The physical environment and its resources place limits on economic growth, as reported already in the early 1970s by the authors of *Limits to Growth*. (Meadows et al. 1972). But they also provide incentives for economic innovation. Technological advances stimulate economic growth. On the other hand, economic investment in technology and education, part of economic change, promotes forward steps in technology which in turn promotes economic growth and might solve environmental and resource depletion problems as technology and know-how advance. Would technology prevail so that solutions are found to the 'limits to growth' in the years and decades to come? Or is the 'technology optimism' unjustified when population increase, industrial output, pollution, natural disasters, resource constraints and other global and regional trends start to interact on a more dramatic scale and at a more rapid pace than at present? These are the major unknowns of the future.

Arrow 6 (b), The Impact of the Changes in the Physical Environment and Technology on Ideological Change and Vice Versa. Will the Debates on the Viability of Continuous Economic Growth and the Dangers of Technology Re-emerge?

The emergence of ecological disasters and signs of global warming created the concept of 'sustainable development' which gave values and a code of conduct for a new kind of ecologically-sensitive development. But if old values are not enough to prevent the deteriorating trends, will these values be questioned, including the almost universal belief in continuous and infinite economic growth? Will alternative belief systems be created to better fit the realities of the 21st century?

Regarding technology's impact on ideology the possibility that terrorists with extreme ideologies would acquire the know-how for building nuclear, biological and chemical weapons, or less powerful tools such as dirty bombs, will increase over time. A new phenomenon in terrorism has been the emergence of ideologically-oriented suicide bombers which might cause more damage as the power of detonation increases through the spread of technology. Any major success might, once again, also attract more attention and more followers.

Arrow 6 (c), The Impacts of the Changes in the Physical Environment and Technology on International System Change and Vice Versa. Will the Question of Improving the Efficiency of the World´s Environmental Management Intensify?

After ominous trends in environmental degradation and the depletion of the earth's resources were recognized in 1960s the international community had to find organizational responses to environmental threats. After the Stockholm Conference on the Human Environment in 1972 a multitude of global and regional environmental agencies, the most prominent being the UN Environmental Programme (UNEP), were created as well as other conference mechanisms. However, if the global and environmental problems, including those related to energy intensify the question will be asked why the current international decision-making system is unable to change negative environmental trends. The challenge is then to identify the key decision-makers regarding environmental deterioration and change the corresponding decision-making patterns – another major challenge for the future.

In terms of the impact of technological change on the international system, technological advances have made internationally standardized elections and polls possible, and immediate news reporting on human rights violations and corruption have become part of global accountability, transparency and international law as almost everywhere in the globe people can have rapid access to breaking news. But the same applies to environmental threats as well. Almost every day there is news about global and regional climate change. These trends will gradually increase the pressure on international and regional decision-making to make more drastic adjustments. If 'things really go bad' the previously-tried reactions of the international community to organize global conferences or create new regulatory bodies on the environment might not be a sufficient response any more. The search for new global and regional responses should therefore intensify, which is an issue to be discussed in the last section of this essay.

Concluding Remarks on the Framework

Ideally, the major trends elaborated upon in this essay – globalization, democratization, regionalism, the increased need for multilateralism and the prevention of global and regional threats – should be discussed jointly, at the same forum, through the same mechanisms and by all stakeholders involved, for maximum efficiency. Whether this kind of discussion on the trends and responses required to counter global and regional threats will become part of the international agenda and decision-making process is yet another set of the unknowns about the future.

A question could also be asked which force in figure 5.1 is 'running the world system'? Is it the economy, technology, environment, education or ideology – or networks as some futurologists claim? As the framework is a dynamic, cybernetic system the question is not that relevant. It is rather the combined effects in which we are interested. As there are hundred of potential factors involved the key is to select only some major variables in order to show the broad trends. One cannot easily see the 'global forest' through the 'local trees'; a broader picture is crucial – the details could be filled in later.

A Global Early Warning and Response System

Quantifying Conceptual Frameworks

After we have built a comprehensive framework for describing major global trends and threats the question of how this framework should be applied in practice with a credible and positive impact on the world arises.

A traditional approach in predicting the future over the past decades has been the creation of monitoring systems or frameworks based on scientific theories and conceptualisations in different sectors of human life – whether in economic, social or environmental fields. In some cases the theories were sophisticated as were Keynesian macroeconomic theories forming the basis of national accounting. In other cases a heuristic, conceptual framework sufficed. But in every case there was the internationally and nationally felt need to create frameworks and data gathering methods for forecasting and planning purposes, in other words, for reducing the harmful risks of the future (see table 1 in the annex).

Computer simulations of the future, like those provided to the Club of Rome, can describe the development of a number of variables and relations but they need systematic statistics as a basis for predictions. Missing data has been one of the problems over the decades in making scenarios and forecasting more reliable, more comprehensive in scope and less contested by the users. The lack of internationally acceptable and standardized statistics, on issues such as on globalization's effects, seriously hampers the development of an efficient set of international responses.

The United Nations has played a major role in quantifying economic, social and environmental activities and creating corresponding standardized statistical systems and accounts which are the basis, for example, for all economic projections and comparisons among countries. Prof. Richard Stone received the Nobel Prize in economics in 1984 for his pioneering work in creating a UN system of national accounts (SNA) in the 1940s and 1950s. He also later worked for the UN Statistical Office in developing a similar system for social accounting (see table 1 in annex).

The development and use of SNA and the aggregates derived from the system – the most important being Gross Domestic Product (GDP) – are instructive. The world-wide collection of data according to SNA recommendations has enabled economists to develop the practice of forecasting into a powerful tool. With the help of national input-output tables and economic models, such forecasting constitutes the basis of today's economic and financial decision-making. For instance, the budget deficit reduction strategies of the U.S. (the country with the greatest impact on the future of global economy), plus strategies in any other country, are based on SNA-based economic forecasts. Critics might question global warming data but they hardly ever criticize – rightly or wrongly – the reliability of GDP and economic growth figures as a basis for major policy decisions.

The basic economic model behind the SNA is relatively simple. O.E. Niitamo (1978) describes it as follows:

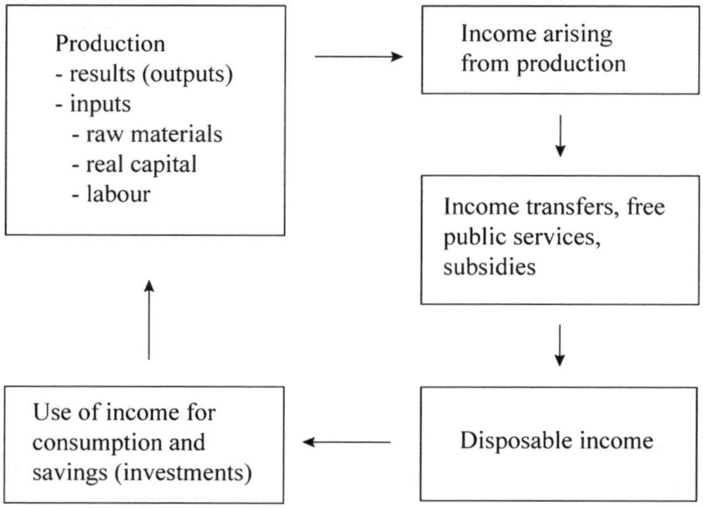

Figure 5.2 The cycle of the system of national accounts

The near phenomenal success of the application of an economic theory to quantify and forecast economic activities led to similar efforts in other fields; from social and environmental to political monitoring. Those earlier efforts over the decades are summarized in table 5.1 in the annex, which was prepared already in 1989 (Kanninen 1989, annex). The development of the Human Development Index, published by the UNDP since 1993, was a later illustration of the continuous application of monitoring, quantification and standardization trends in the UN system.

In order to fill the gap in table 1 of the annex regarding political activity I presented the following overall framework for monitoring political activity at the International Studies Associations Convention in London in March 1989. (Kanninen 1989, 30). It was based on a careful review of the relevant political science literature. At the same time, efforts were taken in the political sector of the UN to build a more sophisticated system of monitoring political events.[14]

14 In a major reform of the political sector of the UN in 1988, Secretary-General Perez de Cuellar established the Office for the Research and the Collection of Information (ORCI) to assist him in his political functions. Dr. James Jonah, first head of ORCI and a graduate of the Massachusetts Institute of Technology established contacts with MIT professors Lincoln P. Bloomfield and Hayward Alker to enlist their support in creating a modern data system for the Office and the UN. Dr. Peter Brecke, Alker's student, now professor at Georgia Tech, was hired for the job. But the proposed system was not implemented as the UN was not ready for using more sophisticated methods. Alker also chaired the panel at the 1989 London ISA Convention for which the above paper was commissioned. Prof. Howard Adelman from York University, Canada, was at the same time also separately assisting in ORCI's early

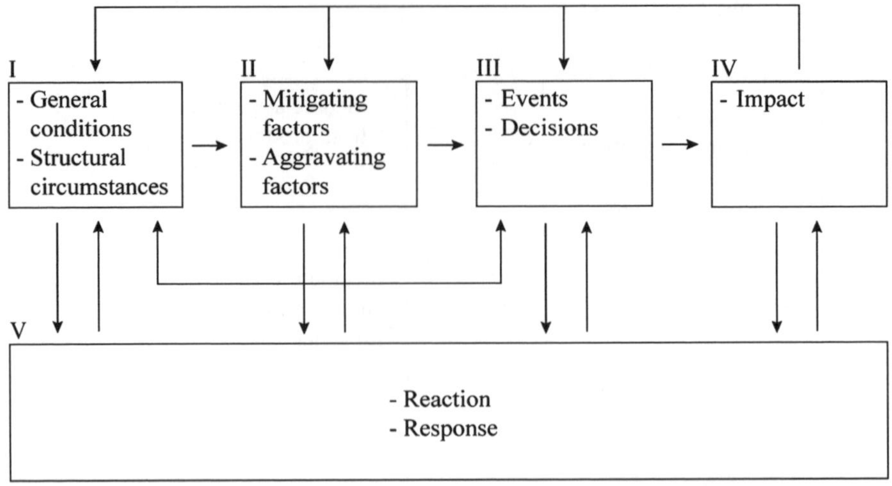

Figure 5.3 A conceptual framework for political monitoring[15]

All the boxes in figure 5.3 are explained in the ISA paper and box III looks as follows:

warning efforts (see footnote 15) and was later involved in developing the early warning and response system for IGAD – explained in the next section of this essay. In 1993, another unsuccessful effort for an integrated political data system was tried for political, peacekeeping and humanitarian departments. The third proposal for an integrated information system was made by an outside body, the so called Brahimi Panel on UN Peace Operations with the same kind of result. However, recently the General Assembly has become more positive about these efforts (see Kanninen and Kumar 2005).

15 The basic framework had some similarities to the model developed by the Refugee Crisis project at York University, Canada, under the leadership of Prof. Howard Adelman and Prof. Michael Lanphier. Their model drew upon Neil Smelser's work on the development of social movements. A 'value added' (a term borrowed from SNA) technique is applied, in which each element (conduciveness, belief, strain) adds to the one previously enunciated until finally the refugee movement is brought to its control stage. If an element is missing, the incipient movement is stalled and or aborted. Likewise, the sequence is incremental. Source: Seminar at York University, April 15, 1988.

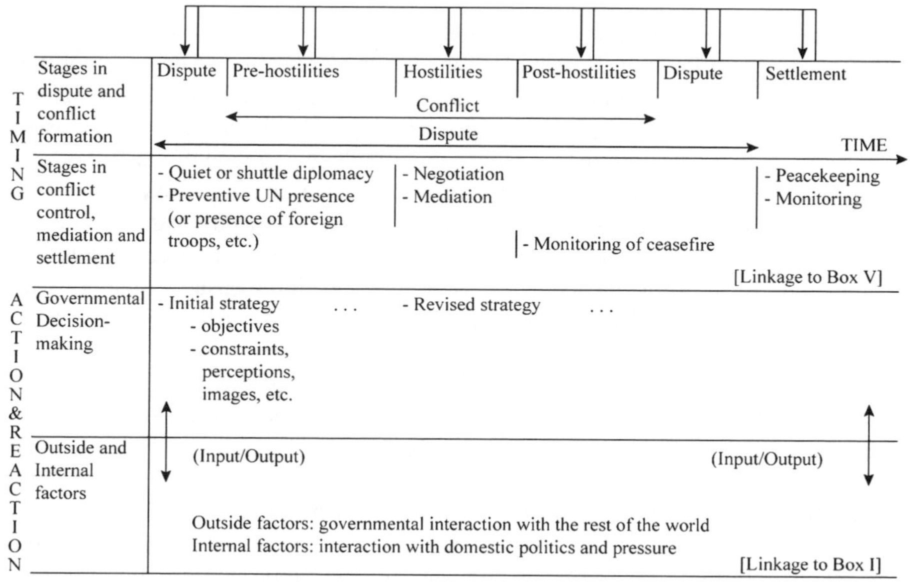

Figure 5.4 The situational analysis of conflicts[16]

In the 1990s a number of efforts indeed took place to create conceptual frameworks and monitoring systems for political activity. This meant, for instance, the development of indicators, checking lists and templates for political analysis. A specific model of the conflict cycle, combining the work of a number of earlier efforts and close to the framework described in figures 5.3 and 5.4, was used as a base for creating an early warning system for two regional organizations as discussed in the next section. (See Mwaura and Schmeidl 2002). At the same time, national governments, corporations and international organizations started to use more sophisticated political risk analysis methods and peace and security related commercial databanks, newswire research engines and special services (such as Lexus, Oxford Analytica, Economist Intelligence Unit, NewsEdge). More sophistication in global modelling and the monitoring of events also increased.[17] Innovations in technology helped in the creation of easily available online databanks about current events.

Still, in political analysis and advice work, we have had great difficulties in bringing the field a step further – in creating an effective political response system for data gathering and analysis as was done for the economy and some other areas. Part of the problem is the 'time' factor, for example the necessity to react instantly to rapidly evolving events; the 'urgency-mode-of-action' usually has no such luxury as to be able to allow for much strategic planning and analysis based on carefully

16 Kanninen 1989, 35.

17 Dr. Doug Bond from Harvard University has been leading the efforts for creating such events based data systems for some UN departments and agencies as well as for IGAD, ECOWAS and the African Union; see also Bold and Meier 2005.

compiled data.

The experience at the UN and elsewhere showed, in the 1980s and onwards, that although the quantification, systematisation and standardisation of data is important for political decision-making, it is less important than to guarantee that whatever analysis was done it is used in decision-making. The linkages between *data-gathering – early warning-analysis – decision-making – action* are still works in progress. Much in political decision-making is by its very nature based on intuition, individual experience, the personal advice of trusted aides, political urgency and the availability of news reports. An additional challenge is to find quick solutions to sudden political problems and at the same time develop measures to address the structural causes of conflicts. (Kanninen and Kumar 2005). All of this has to be coordinated in the bureaucratic environment of large organizations.

How to present an early warning, analysis and prognosis in a clear simple, understandable and 'actionable' manner to decision-makers has therefore been a key issue. A new publication 'Human Security Report 2005', published by the Human Security Centre of the University of British Columbia, closely following the tradition started by the UNDP's Human Development Report.[18] It gathered research and statistics made by political scientists and presented the results in an understandable, non-scientific format – for politicians, scholars and the public at large – thus breaking new ground for systematic political reporting. An annual Global Monitoring Report by the World Bank and IMF, started in 2004, is another effort in the same tradition – in this case to monitor progress in attaining Millennium Development Goals.

Human Development and Security Reports, and Global Monitoring Reports, the innovations of the last 16 years targeting wider and politically important audiences, were to an extent based on earlier quantification efforts in the social sciences, social indicator publications of the 1970s and 1980s and the 'level of living' work of the UN Research Institute for Social Development (UNRISD).[19] While the Global Monitoring Report has as its target audience a Ministerial-level Development Committee of the World Bank and IMF the other two reports do not have a direct, immediate and regular linkage to global and regional decision-making, a major deficiency in addressing the challenges of the future. In addition, the Global Monitoring Report addresses a much more limited number of global issues than suggested in this essay.

Conclusions: Consolidating the Early Experience of Building Monitoring Frameworks

The conceptual framework presented at the beginning of this paper for global and regional monitoring is multidisciplinary and heuristic. It is a combination of the theories and conceptualisations of previous decades. It includes parameters related to changes in values, ideology and culture which have not been part and parcel of

18 Although the report is not a UN publication it was developed by the first Director of the UN Secretary-General's Strategic Planning Unit, Prof. Andrew Mach, with a lot of input from his former colleagues.

19 The UNDP has published Human Development Reports since 1990 and the Human Development Index since 1993.

earlier frameworks. Gradually its items and relationships should be systematised and even quantified and an indicator type of publication could be published based on the framework. What it still needs and needs more than anything is for a political response system to have a real impact on the world. But first there has to be a real need to create such a response system for global and regional trends. These are the questions to be discussed in the last section of this essay.

Building Up a Comprehensive Global Response System

In countering the emerging threats of the 21st century it is not necessary to create a very sophisticated theory and highly detailed monitoring system. Rather, the challenge is to create a relatively simple conceptual framework for explaining basic global and regional variables and their relations; and secondly, to gather data and serious scientific research according to the framework's variables and relations. But the most difficult challenge is to present this, in a very understandable form, to busy political decision-makers and the public at large and ensure that it makes a political impact. Otherwise, it can not be called a political response system at all.

I call this new system a 'comprehensive global early warning and response system'. Some interesting partial efforts have been ongoing in various disciplines and parts of the world to create such a system. This trend already augurs well for eventual success.

In a rudimentary form, a good local early warning-response system is weather forecasting. Predictions are made, then effectively broadcast to the public and we subsequently adjust our clothing for the day. A hurricane forecasting system is a regional application of the concept. On the national scale, another effective early warning-response system is the issuance of official national forecasts of economic growth and other economic variables, based on the System of National Accounts (SNA), and the immediate political response received. SNA-based aggregates are the basis for budget deficit reduction strategies, the decisions on mortgage rates and other economic measures. The SNA also makes international comparisons possible on variables such as economic growth and GDP/capita. When published, they have a broad and immediate political impact in national capitals across regions.

To cite other examples of effective early warning-response systems, the Food and Agricultural Organization (FAO) has a food security early warning system. With regard to natural disasters, new warning systems are being developed in the aftermath of the tsunami in Asia of December 2004. Immediate action based on an early warning is a must in each case.

In the political field two African subregional organizations, IGAD (The Inter-Governmental Authority on Development in East Africa) and ECOWAS (The Economic Community of West African States) have taken steps to institute interesting, even ground-breaking political early warning-response systems in their regions. In both systems civil society and independent research institutions have a major role to play. Civil society monitors collect early warning data, feed it to decision-makers and political authorities immediately react. In the ECOWAS case, civil society actors also take independent preventive action based on same early warning.

In the case of the Conflict Early Warning and Response Mechanism of IGAD, the system (CEWARN) is designed to monitor and analyse pastoral conflicts with the aim of providing early warning on the escalation of violence along with recommendations for action. The development of CEWARN started with cross-border early warning and management along the borders of Ethiopia, Kenya and Somalia. Success was only possible when all actors – including local and national authorities and civil society – worked together. (Mwaura and Schmeidl 2002, Bond and Meier 2005).

For the functioning of the system each IGAD Member State is required, through the decisions of the Governments of the regions, to establish a CEWARN Unit. The units are composed jointly of the government, the military, non-governmental organizations and research institutions. Their functions are to verify, analyse and comment on information coming from independent field monitors. A central unit located in Addis Ababa acts as a clearing house and manages a database and Internet communication centre. At the highest political level, the system is coordinated by the 'Permanent Secretaries Steering Committee' of IGAD Member States Governments. An important feature of the system is its immediate linkage to decision-makers in IGAD countries and IGAD's Executive Secretary. The early warning system has already been used to respond to potential conflicts at local levels.

While CEWARN has so far only covered rural conflicts, ECOWAS has more ambitious plans including reporting on such incidences as governance collapse, human rights violations, small arms proliferation and conflicts over resources. A new system is also being built on the interplay between governments and civil society.

In the summit of Lome in 1999 the heads of State and Governments of ECOWAS first adopted a protocol for conflict prevention and established four subregional centers (zonal bureaus) and the Observation and Monitoring Centre at ECOWAS headquarters in Abuja for a new early warning and response system. The field monitors are independent civil society representatives (selected by the West African Network for Peacebuilding, WANEP) who periodically send their field reports to four zonal bureaus. These subregional centres have both civil society and governmental representatives. The information is analysed by the staff of the bureaus and submitted to the Abuja Center at ECOWAS headquarters. But civil society also has an independent information centre in Accra and could initiate preventive action independently from governments. It might also issue press releases to the media. WANEP is already actively using the early warning system to head off disputes at the local level.[20]

But the biggest challenge of today and tomorrow goes beyond any single regional and political conflict. A daunting task is to create an effective political early warning-response system to address global and regional threats to humankind as described in this essay and other pertinent literature. Such a body of literature is already vast

---

20 'Conflict Prevention and Peacebuilding in the Regional Context', a seminar organized by the UN University's Comparative Regional Integration Studies programme and the UN Department of Political Affairs in Bruges, Belgium on 28-29 April 2006; presentations by Colonel Kone Yoro of ECOWAS, Jacop Eben-Enoh from WANEP and Prof. Doug Bond from Harvard University; see <http://www.cris.unu.edu/admin/documents/20060901153539.O-2006-20.pdf.>

and expanding but also confusing as there are no organizing principles to summarize disjointed data and key findings gathered by public and private agencies, research institutions, corporations and the media.

The 1972 book *Limits to Growth* opened with the quotation by UN Secretary-General U Thant. (Meadows et al. 1972):

> I do not wish to seem overdramatic, but I can only conclude from the information that is available to me as Secretary-General, that the Members of the United Nations have perhaps ten years left in which to subordinate their ancient quarrels and launch a global partnership to curb the arms race, to improve human environment, to defuse the population explosion and to supply the required momentum to development efforts. If such a global partnership is not forged with the next decade, then I very much fear that the problems I have mentioned will have reached such staggering proportions that they will be beyond our capacity to control.

In the '*30 Year Update to Limits to Growth*' Donella and Dennis Meadows and Jorgen Randers concluded that this global partnership is not in evidence. They say that the highly aggregate scenarios of the original model – showing drastic global disruptions in areas such as the economy, population, industrial output, pollution and resources starting in the years from 2010 to 2030 – still appear after 30 years to be surprisingly accurate, and better supported by the data and examples that have been gathered since 1972. Humanity is in overshoot and the authors offer a wealth of data and analysis that contradicts prevailing political pronouncements that mankind is on the correct path for its twenty-first century. Whatever lies ahead, the authors say, its main dimensions will emerge over the next two decades. The global economy is already so far above sustainable levels that, they claim, there will be little time left for the fantasy of an infinite globe. The authors concluded that the adjustment will be a huge task entailing a 'revolution as profound as the agricultural and industrial revolutions'. (Meadows et al. 2004).

Whether we believe this group of scientists – and many do because of the deepening climate changes all over the world – or any other group what we badly need is more information and projections dealing with global and regional trends. And, most importantly, we need a new system forcing the global decision-makers – whether politicians, corporate executives, world opinion leaders or builders of international networks – to make regular adjustments (sometimes gradual ones and in other cases drastic ones) to change the course before it is too late.

At the moment the world has a rather haphazard global early warning –response system of reporting, discussing and acting on global and regional threats – whether political, economic, social, humanitarian or environmental – and even less of a system regarding their interaction and the multidisciplinary solutions required to address them before they spin out of control.
We have more or less every year:

1. Periodic global commissions, panels or high-level working groups on sectoral issues and challenges (disarmament, the environment, UN reforms, or on special occasions such as the millennium celebration). The reports of these eminent groups and bodies are issued practically every year in one form or

another. There is subsequently some discussion at the UN, in regional agencies or at policy or academic conferences and then each issue moves gradually to the background, re-emerges, disappears, and the cycle goes on;

2. Periodic sectoral UN reports or publications such as the UNDP's Human Development Reports, the World Bank´s reports, UN Economic Surveys. These reports are usually discussed by the UN and regional bodies, benchmarks of a long standing tradition but without a deep impact on international or national decision-making.

The publication of the following reports and related newscasts has even less systematic and long-term follow-up by the international community:

1. Periodic reports and newsletters by policy or scientific institutes such as Amnesty International, Human Rights Watch, the International Crisis Group and climate change panels and institutes;

2. Periodic reports by governmental agencies on human rights, the status of the arms trade, terrorism, the environment and many other fields;

3. Media reports on TV, radio and in newspapers on global and regional threats; and

4. Articles, books and movies on the same.

The major problems are that:

1. The discussion and search for solutions about global and regional threats are both dispersed, ad hoc and short-term – moving from one popular issue to another, from one year's issue to another;

2. The setting of the agenda of the world´s attention regarding global problems is basically government-driven in which national interests dominate;

3. There is no systematic way for the international community to understand and project the interactions of the world´s problems and see the interdependent world from a long-term perspective – as a comprehensive, interconnected system;

4. There is no credible way for the international community to find out what the most urgent threats are, particularly if the earth and its regions' carrying capacities in some areas is approaching, or has passed, the limits of no-return and

5. The reaction of the international community to emerging threats is delayed as there is no broad agreement on the validity and reliability of critical data (such as on global warming); this problem calls for urgent efforts to internationally

standardize statistics, research findings and monitoring systems on global and regional trends.

A Possible Solution

Based on the earlier discussions of lessons learned in creating early warning and response systems in various fields and regions, there might be a possible way to proceed in establishing an effective monitoring and reaction system to counter regional and global threats. The experience of IGAD and ECOWAS, for instance, shows that an intergovernmental organization and civil society organizations and research institutions can work closely together to create and implement an efficient early warning and response system.

One solution, but only one, is to institute a yearly report from an independent, rotating group of high-ranking scientists of a multidisciplinary background as an annex to the UN Secretary-General's Annual Report on the Work of the Organization. It could be entitled: *Global and Regional Threats, their Interaction and Solutions* or just *Global Report*. The Secretary-General should have no control over the results of the work of the group but he or she could and should ask various parts of the UN system, and regional and other bodies, to comment on the findings and ask how their work is affected by the analyses and scenarios of the future.

The Annual Report of the Secretary-General is one of the most important – if not the most important – regular reports of the UN. Mentioned in the Charter as the only report the Secretary-General has to prepare it defines his/her leadership of the Organization.[21] Diplomats study it carefully as do decision-makers in capitals and its publication in early September usually hits the headlines in the media. Secretary-General Kofi Annan started a new practice by introducing it to the General Assembly in person shortly before the U.S. President speaks ensuring maximum world media attention. Afterwards the report is debated by the General Assembly. But until now it has not led to any immediate effects and certainly not long-term major policy changes by the international community.

The role of the Annual Report and its Annex could change if the Secretary-General intends to promote and expand its role in UN decision-making. In addition to the debates in the media and recommendations of the General Assembly the Secretary-General has the right to bring such matters in the report that threaten international peace and security to the attention of the Security Council, according to Article 99 of the Charter. If the Council acts, the decisions of the Council are binding and have a high degree of legitimacy. The Security Council has recently moved beyond strictly political issues to discuss areas such as HIV/AIDS.

The benefits of the proposed system might be that:

1. Top scientists would gradually start to contribute more seriously than before to the shaping of the world´s agenda bringing the attention of decision-makers

21 Article 98 of the UN Charter: …'The Secretary-General shall make an annual report to the General Assembly on the work of the Organization.'

to global and regional threats – both short-term, medium and long-term – and their interactions in the future and the measures required to alleviate them;

2. As the scientists would change every year each report would have a surprise element which would both attract attention and make sure that no school of thought would dominate the findings of the report;

3. As the scientists are independent both from the UN and governments one could be relatively confident that the quality of analysis would be high and not dominated by national interests;

4. Although the results might not affect the agenda of the international community, corporations, media and ordinary citizens in the short term, the ensuing debates by politicians, diplomats, corporate leaders, media and civil society might change priorities in the medium and long term and bring more seriousness to the search for solutions to global and regional problems;

5. An important side effect might be the initiation of a project to internationally standardize data and research methodology in the most critical areas so that disagreements on data and research findings would not sabotage efforts to find effective solutions to most urgent and persistent threats.

The foreseen change of the proposed early warning-response system would be a gradual move away from the world's media driven agenda-setting, which at the moment focuses on immediate events (for example the chain reaction: *rapidly evolving events – reporting by media – reaction from decision-makers – new media analyses – reaction by politicians – a series of decisions are taken*).[22] What we need is a new kind of agenda-setting where immediate events – no matter how tragic they might be – would not totally overshadow and sap the energy from efforts to address the longer term threats and their interactions.

The conceptual model presented in the first section of this essay gives a tentative framework as well as an agenda for the threats to be discussed in the preparation of the global report, it also has a high degree of flexibility, and might help in giving guidance for the collection of information, statistics and research – or the undertaking of new studies – to support the work of the eminent scientists' group. Computer

22 On logistics: The setting up of a group of scientists could be an initiative solely taken by the UN Secretary-General. He or she would have full authority under the UN Charter to do so, namely to prepare the annual report in any way, regarding content and logistics he or she would like to. At least in its the beginning and to make sure that the group was taken seriously, some of the scientists could be Nobel laureates or of similar quality and name-recognition. The group could have an advisory board that would have scientific associations or institutes as its members. The funding for the necessary research, analysis and logistics should become from various sources in order to guarantee the independent nature and quality of the undertaking.

simulations of the future interaction of key variables might also be helpful for stimulating public debate. In addition to any *annual overview of global and regional progress or decline*, one or two issues could be reviewed in more detail in a given year.

The report would have some resemblance, as a global response, to the social reports and social indicator publications that national authorities started to prepare in the 1970s in order to give a holistic picture of the achievements, shortcomings and challenges of governmental policies. Those publications were not made by independent scientists but governmental agencies. Independence from governmental agendas – or from the parochial agendas of the researchers for that matter – is the key for the system proposed here. Secondly, earlier social reports were not prepared annually as there was no need for such regularity. But the severity of global and regional threats and the need for the earliest possible responses might indeed require a yearly reporting and response system.

An Alternative Proposal

Another alternative is to use an existing organization or to create a new institution without direct links to the UN, headed by a world-class statesman/woman or a small group of former leaders and other eminent personalities or scholars, with easy access to the world´s media and decision-makers. The annual agenda, research capacity and the mission of the institution could be the same as in the above proposal. A possible problem with this alternative is that it would not formally be part of the annual political decision-making cycle of the international system, as the proposal above would be. But it still might be a way to start the incremental process, through experimenting with various options, by conducting research on threats and short and longer term measures and mechanisms to address them. Gradually, it might have a more serious impact on the world's decision-making processes, including direct linkages to the UN, regional and other intergovernmental and non-governmental organizations.

If the dangers explained by many scientists and practitioners facing the international community in the years and decades to come are true the world urgently needs a new comprehensive system for addressing the threats on a regular, annual basis. The key would be to start the process of thinking about and experimenting with various alternatives and solutions. This essay has provided a conceptual framework, an agenda, plus two options for proceeding forward.

The views presented in this essay are those of the author and do not necessarily represent those of the United Nations.

Annex: International efforts to standardize the description and measurement of the 'realities' of appropriate decades (Kanninen 1989)

Decade	Historical origins	International measurement response	Theories in the background	International agencies responsible	National agencies responsible
1940-1950	- To avoid 1930's types of depressions - To correct economic imbalances - To facilitate growing international trade and other economic relations	- SNA + System of Material Balances - Input/output models - Econometric models	- Keynes' theories (+ Marxist production theories) - Richard Stone's work - etc	- UN Statistical Office (- OECD, CMEA) (- WB, IMF)	- Statistical agencies - Economic Ministries - Universities, research centres
1960-1970	- To control social instability - To improve living standard and fight against poverty - To solve problems in labor markets, migration, population growth etc	- System of Social and Demographic Statistics - Social indicator movement - Standard of living measurements - Social reporting	- Richard Stone's work (life cycles) - Theories of basic human needs - etc	- UN Statistical Office - UNRISD, ILO - ECE (- UNESCO) (- OECD, CMEA)	- Statistical agencies - National agencies dealing with social issues - Universities, research centres
1970-1980	- To control international pollution - To avoid depletion of resources - To predict and avoid ecological catastrophes	- Framework for Environmental Statistics - System of Materials and Energy Balances - Earthwatch, Infoterra - Club of Rome-types global models	- Environmental Stress-Response Models - Engineering models of pollution and energy/ materials flows - etc	- UNEP - UN Statistical Office - ECE (- UNITAR)	- Environmental agencies - Statistical agencies - Universities, research centres
1980-	- All of the above and: - To avoid nuclear war (between superpowers or regional rivals) - To prevent and predict conflicts, especially with escalation potential - Avoid and control nuclear and other terrorist acts				

Chapter 6

Platforms, Pieces and Probabilities – Introducing the 3P-Model[1]

Mika Aaltonen

Introduction

This chapter focuses on the macro-level transformation of societies. The main theories that present societal change from a general perspective are presented and evaluated from three analytical views: time reference, continuity and the dynamics of change. After the analysis, the origins, methods and insights into the emergence and immergence of the future, of arguably the most experienced, far-sighted and accurate observer of our world; John Naisbitt, are reviewed, and out of all those elements the 3P (Platforms, Pieces and Probabilities) - Model has been sketched.

How Societies Change?

Arguably, the eight best-known theories of societal transformation are: modernity, cycle theory, historical capitalism, the global age, post-modernity, reflexive modernity, the information age and the hydrogen economy (c.f. Kuosa 2005). I present a brief summary of them below as together they form a solid basis from which it is possible to reflect upon and evaluate the 3P-Model.

These theories are not necessarily unified entities, but rather collections of ideas, assumptions, and even ideologies that provide unique and recognizable points of view on societal change. There are many complementary and contradictory issues and approaches to each of these theories that remain outside my focus. My intention has been to clarify the specific features that distinguish the theories from each other and give them an identity with respect to time reference, continuity and the dynamics of change.

The first two theories presented here – modernity and cycle theory – share a long time span, perhaps with modernity the time span is infinite, and both theories prefer continuity to discontinuity.

Modernity can be described as a typically linear theory. It relies on the continuous convergence of societies, stability and order; and the formative forces of technology, capitalism and nation states. For most of the theorists of modernity (e.g. Berger et al. 1974, Habermas 1987, Giddens 1990 and 1991, Bauman 1998) there exist only more

1 Intellectual debt to discussions with and presentations of the world-renowned futurist John Naisbitt is acknowledged. Nevertheless, the views expressed in this chapter are those of the author and do not necessarily reflect the total position of John Naisbitt.

or less advanced modern societies; thus all societies can be presented in the time continuum of modernisation. Modernisation is comprehended as a process, where technology drives economic growth and development; and advancement works as a movement towards a fuller rationalisation.

The origins of cycle theory are often traced back to The World Economy and its Condition During and After War (1922); a doctoral thesis by Russian Nikolai D. Kondratieff. He could be described as a great believer in hindsight; he insisted that future economic trends can be predicted from past economic periods. According to Kondratieff national economies alternate in 50 year long period cycles, where one period of economic recession is followed by a period of economic growth and so on. Inside the long cycles, there are mid to long cycles of 7 to 10 years, and short cycles of 3 to 4 years. Moreover, in each long period cycle there will be one or more catalysts or engines, which will enable the entry of a new cycle. (Mager 1987). Despite a general intellectual reluctance to accept that economic forces run in preordained, mechanistic cycles Kondratieff's theory has won many supporters and been a source for many modified applications e.g. Toffler's wave metaphor (1981), Yakovet's cycles of civilization (1993), and Elliott's waves in finance and social dynamics (Frost and Prechter and Collins 1999).

In contrast to the above historical capitalism and the global age theories predict a clear cut with the past.

Immanuel Wallerstein (1974, 1983) assumes that historical capitalism was brought into being in the 16th century, which led to Europe eventually becoming a global phenomenon in the 19th century[2]. Its foundations can be condensed into three propositions: the use of capital to generate new capital, the restriction of competition to gain advantage, and the establishment of world markets. In contrast to the two previously presented theories, that (in general) see the positive evolution of a better world and the continuous convergence of world markets, Wallerstein argues that there will be an increasing polarization that leads to an abject proletariat, and finally to the end of modernisation. Thereafter a new society will be formed based on a new form of socialism, which will have mentally, and physically new foundations and new formative forces.

Global age theory anticipates a whole new era not due to the collapse of capitalism as historical capitalism does, but due to the growing gap between generations and the unique expansion of globalization, this explanation shares a kinship with the argumentation of the information age theory, in which the emergence of the future is seen as an independent, non-deterministic, unstable process, which cannot be halted. (Albrow 1997).

Post-modernity and reflexive modernity share similar qualities and they might be considered to be kinship theories as they concentrate on present and near future.

However, the idea of discontinuity between the eras of modernity and post-modernity is pinpointed in post-modern writing. Instead of linear development and the general expansion of goods and ideas the thematic emphasis lies on increased relativism, ambivalence, contingency, and qualitative diversity; as well as the fragmentation of ideas into ever smaller units that have little in common. (Scott 1997, Bauman 1998).

2 The comparisons between Immanuel Wallerstein's theory and Karl Marx's Historical Materialism can be read in Wallerstein 1983.

From these intellectual elements we could conclude that post-modernity is a complex, but robust phenomena that includes the idea of self-organization. A post-modern society is a far from equilibrium system, it is in constant state of flux, and able to organise itself in new, previously non-existent ways and levels.

Reflexive modernity differs from post-modernity most of all when they are compared with respect to continuity. While post-modernists assume that a major disruption of structures will take place as a consequence of moving eras from modernity to post-modernity; reflexive modernists take the view that the transition will be smooth, known and conscious. (Beck 1986, Giddens 1990, Giddens 1991, Beck and Giddens and Lask 1994). Such a paradigm shift is also seen as introducing new forms of capitalism, politics and laws regarding how nation states influence the world community.

The last two theories presented here are the information age and the hydrogen economy.

For one of the most prolific information age writer, Manuel Castells (1996, 1997, 1998), the coupling of the ICT revolution and an expanding network economy represents a break between the modern era and the forthcoming era. He argues that modern production modes, structures and social classes will fade because in the information age people will be divided into classes based on their relationship to the Internet, and not to modes of production as they were before.

With regard to the hydrogen economy a recent point of reference at theory level was provided by Jeremy Rifkin (2002) when in his *Hydrogen Economy* he argued that the macro-level transformation of societies has always depended on their position with respect to energy. In the 19th century coal and steam were the suppliers of energy, in the 20th century it was oil, and in the 21st century it will be hydrogen followed by various impacts on economic, political, social, and environmental issues. The argumentation has a similar logic in its theory of change to that of Manuel Castell's information age argument – the change is seen to depend on a single factor; except here the Internet is replaced by energy.

Detecting Patterns

Finding time to read the huge amounts of papers, articles, reports and books that might be professionally helpful is a challenge. Finding meaning in the overwhelming flow of bits and pieces of information is an even bigger challenge.

In the movie *Beautiful Mind* the mathematician, and later also a Nobel-prize winner, John Nash was shown standing puzzled in his working room filled with all sorts of newspapers and journals. He was trying to discover a code the texts might contain, a secret message hidden into pieces of information that alone say very little or nothing at all about the message.

We believe that, detecting patterns, discovering causal linkages between things, events and people which are not obvious usually increases the power, efficacy and accuracy of interventions. In social systems patterns are not always complex, they can also be relatively simple, yet unknown to us. However, every time a new pattern that fits the behaviour of the system is discovered, it is likely to benefit the discoverer.

Generally patterns are needed to reveal previously large, complicated or complex issues in ways that we can understand. When we observe, reason and understand the interactions of various agents, flows of information and connections between certain issues we begin to make sense of bits and pieces of information; the existing and emerging patterns. Pattern management requires more than the reading of multi-faceted empirical data. It calls for multiple methods, expertise and resources.

The logic of Amazon.com recommendations is based on simple pattern recognition: the coupling of elements that together make sense of customers' preferences. When entering the web site, you have a book recommendation waiting under which you will find the question: 'Why this is recommended to me?' If you click that line, you will find two more lines. First 'Recommended for you' then the name of a book or books recommended for you; then another line 'Because you purchased' followed by a name or names of books that you have already purchased at Amazon.com. The linkage between your previous purchases has led to certain recommendations, because the customers who have bought the same books you have, have also purchased the recommended books.

The French philosopher Pierre Bourdieu discusses in his *Raisons pratiques. Sur la théorie de l'action* (1994) the complex relationships that describe certain life styles depending on whether people drink champagne, whiskey, mineral water, Pernod, sparkling wine, cheap red wine or beer; whether their hobbies are riding, sailing, bridge, chess, swimming, biking, fishing, belote or football; and what kind of political opinions and jobs they have. Making sense of these patterns is an every day practice for example in consumer behaviour studies, the fashion and clothing industry, and in Internet-related businesses.

A different kind of pattern arises when information is gathered from multiple sources and the outcome of a pattern is detected. For example, purchases of certain chemicals or equipment can lead to the ability to spot whether someone is possibly building or creating something that previously, without the existence of all the necessary building blocks was impossible, e.g. a terrorist attack or building a nuclear weapon.

When I asked John Naisbitt if he had seen *Beautiful Mind*, and if he recalled the above described scene, he replied immediately 'That is exactly how I work!' However, not all the people have the talent, experience and possibilities that John Nash or John Naisbitt has to make sense of the existing and emerging patterns. Making sense of complex situations used to be the privilege of only a few people in the world. Today, large amounts of people need it in their daily practices and it is assisted by sophisticated tools and techniques available to many.

The method, content analysis, which Naisbitt uses, is probably most thoroughly explained in his first book *Megatrends* (1982). The pragmatic goal was to understand what was really happening in the USA by monitoring local events and behaviour, because local behaviour represents what is going on in America.

The origins of the method can be found in World War II. Analyses of German newspapers showed the strain of the war on the German people as problems in industry and the economy begun little by little to show up in its newspapers. For example, there was no general information about soldiers killed, but local papers listed their names, they told stories about the openings and closings of factories and so on. Collecting information about what was going on locally provided the basis for looking for patterns, and the results were insightful.

For *Megatrends* more than 2 million local articles in local newspapers were analysed, at the time it was a laborious job to do, nevertheless the patterns were recognized. Besides the recognition of patterns, an additional insight was produced: trends are generated bottom up, while fads are generated top down.

Pattern management is not a closed discipline with strict systems, procedures and methods. It is the observation of common denominators within various fields of life. In pattern management two philosophical notions guide our efforts: 1) the search for associations and similarities at any level of content or expression; thus the elements need to have something in common, but they do not need to be identical in order to belong to same pattern; 2) the combination of the actors, the order of events and the pieces of information must fit into a convincing narrative, which consists of subject's pursuit of an object, he considers valuable, and the other elements that have or find their roles in this pursuit.

Both notions were embedded in Elias Lönnrot's groundbreaking work *Kalevala* (1835). The Finnish folklorist spent years of his life walking around Carelia, listening and talking to people and writing traditional, orally transmitted stories into his note books. Ultimately, he was able to give them a literary form, creating one of the mightiest epics in the world, which in contrast to many other epics, e.g. *The Iliad* and *The Odyssey* by Homer or *The Lord of the Rings* by J. R. R. Tolkien, is heavily based on the oral tradition of a people rather than the creative work of novelists. (Aaltonen 1997).

Lönnrot's work was strongly grounded in real world effort; on the analysis of a huge amount of data, in which the patterns were detected and meaning was given through the discerning narrative.

Introducing the 3P-Model

People focusing on the macro-level transformation of societies face an ambiguous and hard task. Looking for emerging properties and explanations for emergence is a demanding job even with simple and linear systems, not to mention generative models. This is because the new order in which the pattern produced by the elements of a system, cannot be accounted for in terms of the individual action of any of the individual elements of the system, but rather by the synergism created amongst them. (E.g. Bertuglia and Vaio 2003).

By nature general models are reductive; they are made of choices, preferences and exclusions; certain themes, mechanisms and properties are included, others excluded. Despite the difficulty of the task, not all the attempts at modelling the developments on a general level are equally good, some models work better than others. As Pierre-Simon Laplace in his *Essai philosohique sur les probabilités* (1825) states we should not confuse knowledge with ignorance.

Platforms

For John Naisbitt, the starting point for anticipating the future is the understanding of the present, 'looking at the score board of the game', making sense of what is really happening, because 'the future is embedded in the present'. The 3p–Model consists of three interacting elements that together form the basis for the dynamics of change where everything is either growing or dying: platforms refer to the main drivers of the development and they deal with long time periods. 'The revolution comes in clusters' preceded by long periods of evolution. During the evolutionary periods, there is lots of excitement. However, many weak signals and bubbles are stillborn as none of them can lead to a revolution until a platform is ready. Inside each platform, we can regard the situation as being a jigsaw puzzle with various pieces, in this case: politics, economics, environment, values, society and technology. You may pick up any piece to look at it more carefully, study its relations to other pieces, and then put it back in the puzzle. The double-loop for one´s consideration is provided via two simple conceptual tools: both smaller and larger issues can be evaluated with respect to whether they are expected to change or remain as they are, and they can be evaluated in detail according to the potentiality they represent.[3]

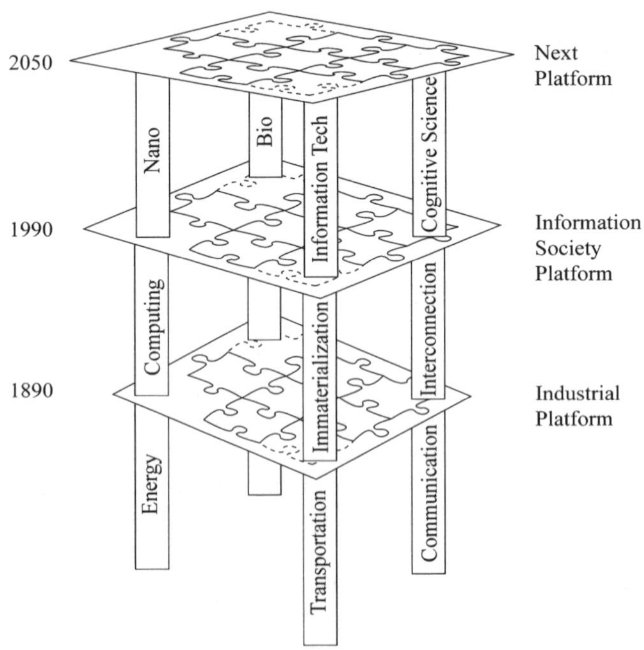

Figure 6.1 The platforms of yesterday, today and tomorrow

Revolutions seldom take place and they always come in clusters. The pieces of the industrial platform finally came together around 1890, when energy, in the form of

3 Expressions used by John Naisbitt.

electricity, transportation, in the form of cars and airplanes, and communication, in the form of radio, were developed far enough to benefit masses of people. The information society boom and bubble were born only after all the pieces coalesced around 1990, when computing, immaterialisation and interconnection were in place in the puzzle. John Naisbitt estimates that we will have to wait until 2050 for the next revolution, which is sometimes called the NBIC. The NBIC revolution consists of the synergies between the new drivers: nano-, bio-, information technology or conscious technology, and the cognitive sciences. These synergies are likely to change the conception of life, we possess today.

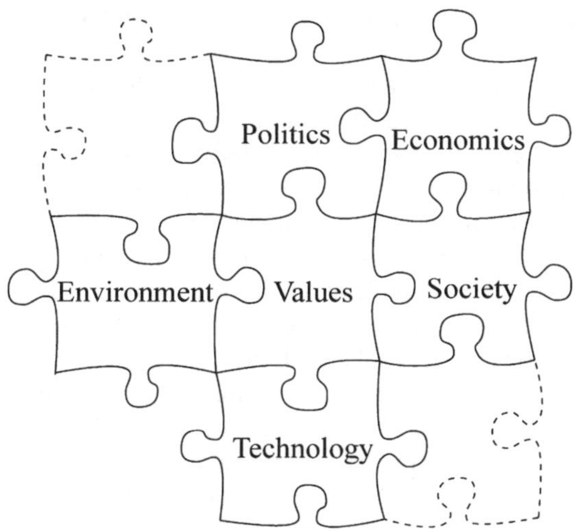

Figure 6.2 Pieces and the puzzle of the future

Pieces

It may be beneficial to see the world as a jigsaw puzzle in which the most important pieces are the geographical, political, economic, societal and technological ones. We can also study the pieces one by one, and also for their interaction and influence on the other pieces. For example Ronald Inglehart's Global Value Survey, would provide us with a point of reference from a value perspective, the Japanese technology foresight study NISTEP would do the same from a technological perspective, Deutsche Bank's *Formel-G* (chapter 4) from an economic perspective et cetera.

We may also reflect on our choice of pieces, whether we should take notice of certain identified issues or other issues not normally identified with the point of reference or pieces that have been taken into consideration by others comparing our jigsaw puzzle to other organizations' puzzles. Below I present the differing ways three recent futures projects have made sense of their respective worlds.

Firstly, the US intelligence project Octagon has called for new instruments on intelligence to deal with the ever more complex world that they review through eight windows: the environment, the biosphere, health and medicine; wealth, finance, business and economics; virtuality, temporality and alternative life; humanities, sociology and philosophy; law, ethics, criminality and alternative cultures; science, engineering and technology; distribution, transportation and networking; and finally through national security and military affairs.

Secondly, Shell Global Scenarios to 2025 discusses specific forces, features and contexts that will impact upon the global business environment as a whole. The three forces that have been chosen as the basis for scenarios are efficiency in the form of market incentives; security created by coercion or regulation; and social cohesion built by the force of community. The forces are seen as driving towards different objectives. However the trade-offs between them shape the descriptions of the world.

Thirdly, McKinsey (Davis and Stephenson 2006) regard that the business landscape as being transformed by ten trends. According to McKinsey three macroeconomic trends will change the global economy: the shift of economic activity centers; the public-sector balloon; and changes in the consumer landscape. Four social and environmental trends will influence how we live and work: the connectivity of technology will change how people live and interact; the battle for talents will become tougher; the role and behaviour of big business will come under increasingly sharp scrutiny; and demand for natural resources will grow. They identify three business and industry trends that will drive changes at the company level: the emergence of new global industry structures; management shift from art to science; and ubiquitous computing, which will change the economics of knowledge.

These considerations all work at the jigsaw puzzle level, share the same time frame and discuss similar forms of change dynamics. They help us to validate our conceptions, but they cannot replace our own work.

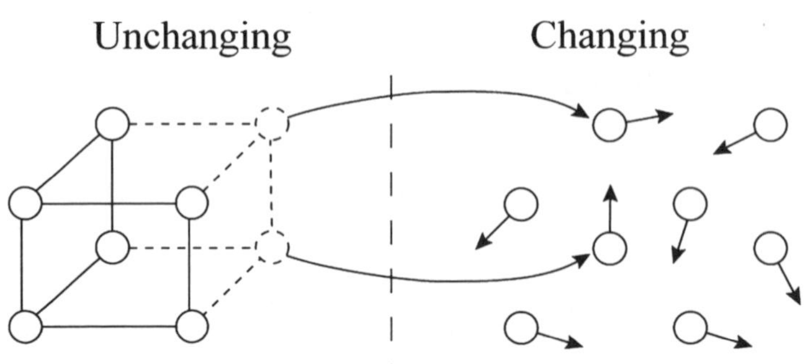

Figure 6.3 Things that will remain unchanged, and things that will change

Probabilities

We can go into more detail in our analysis and evaluate which are the pieces in our analysis that we expect to remain as they are, and things that we expect to change. 'Many pieces of our analysis are changing now, but most of them are not changing at all'. 'Things that are meant to happen always happen more slowly than we expect, and the biggest surprises derive from those pieces that are expected to remain unchanged, but do change'.[4]

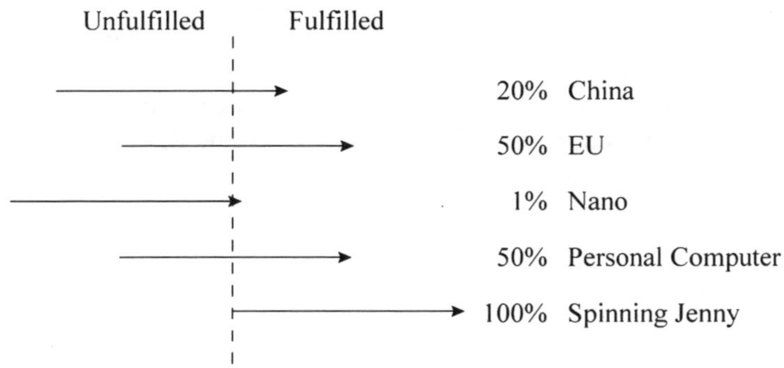

Figure 6.4 The unfulfilled and fulfilled potentiality of the pieces

Inside the jigsaw puzzle one more step is needed to be taken in detail. We can evaluate the existing building blocks according to how much they have realized their potential. For example, the Spinning Jenny has totally fulfilled its potential, we can discuss China and the EU or the personal computer; it is not so clear how much of their potential has been fulfilled, but perhaps the discussion will be helpful even without any agreement on figures, with regard to nanotechnology it is safe to say its potential is mostly unfulfilled.

A Consideration of the 3P-Model

The 3P-Model relies on continuous reflection between various factors and time scales. It takes into account multiple time scales and in this way it most resembles cycle theory, but also modernity and historical capitalism, which have long-term perspectives. Continuity is preferred to discontinuity, and in that way cycle theory, modernity and reflexive modernity are closest to the 3P-Model, while its evolutionary dynamics most resemble those of reflexive modernism with its smooth, known and conscious transition led by new drivers.

In theory building the 3P-Model expresses great simplicity in its premises, clarity in its dynamics, and still it remains open to a wide range of applications. The 3P-Model dynamics emerge out of the platforms that represent a long-term view. Choosing and making sense of the drivers on which long-term development depends is a crucial activity. Inside the platforms, medium-term evolution can be evaluated by using the jigsaw puzzle metaphor. There will be numerous differing opinions on the pieces that should be involved in the puzzle and on the pieces that will most shape our world in the medium-term, not to mention lots of uncertainty

4 Expressions used by John Naisbitt.

about the probable outcomes of their interactions. It is essential such an analysis though, because making sense of the present is the key to understanding the future. Detecting patterns hidden in the huge amount of events and information available in the world lifts the intelligence of our strategic work and reveals which players are in the game, what their roles are in it, what goals are being pursued and lastly, what relationships between various pieces of information are being looked at.

The 3P-Model can be tested and discussed at all its levels and in its time frames; and as a theory, as well as a conceptual entity when we deal with dynamics of change. In essence, the 3P-Model is, above all else, a reflexive model, capable of absorbing and learning from a huge number of sources.

PART 3
Revisiting Casual Theory

Chapter 7

Sensitiveness to Initial Conditions: Reconceptualising Cause

Mika Aaltonen and T. Irene Sanders

Introduction

Sensitiveness to initial conditions is one of the key insights that derive from complex systems theory. In discussing emergence of future, it permits us to rethink the underlying logic of change and to reconceptualise cause. New initial conditions are the changes and developments that are already taking place below the surface. We believe that there is a linkage between certain initial conditions and the success of an organization. This chapter provides an inspirational challenge to sense-making and strategic decision-making: to identify and influence our systems' initial conditions as they are emerging. Preparing ourselves for coming changes by identifying them; and shaping the future to our advantage by influencing them is foresight.

About Social Systems

In the last twenty-five years, rapid advances in high-speed computing and computer graphics have created a revolution in scientists' understanding of complex systems, such as organizations, markets and economies. The same technologies that have given us instant access to news and information from around the world – allowing us to think and act as one vast interconnected system – have made it possible to study the non-linear dynamics of systems that were once hopelessly inaccessible or took years to understand. (Sanders 2003).

Simply stated, complexity is a dynamic quality or pattern of interaction that arises when 'an increasing number of independent variables begin interacting in interdependent and unpredictable ways'. (Ilachinski 2001).

Complexity science represents a growing body of interdisciplinary knowledge about the structure, behaviour and dynamics of change in a specific category of complex systems. Much of the world is comprised of complex *adaptive* systems – open evolutionary systems such as rain forest, a business, a society, our immune systems, the World Wide Web or the rapidly globalizing world economy – where the components are strongly interrelated, self-organizing and dynamic. (Sanders and McCabe 2003).

In recent years, many of the basic characteristics and principles by which complex systems organize, operate and evolve have been identified, leading to important insights and research implications in almost every field. As a result, we are witnessing the integration of knowledge across disciplines and the emergence of new concepts, tools and a new vocabulary. (Turcott and Rundle 2003).

One of the most important notions is that we are moving away from a linear, mechanistic view of the world, to one based on non-linear dynamics, evolutionary development and system thinking (Lorenz 1963, Sanders 1998). This shift represents a dramatic new way of looking at things; not just looking at more things at once.

Extending our understanding of the dynamics of complex systems into the domain of social systems is the new frontier. When understood and used as a sense-making framework, insights from complex systems research can be used to understand and influence complex socio-political systems. (Sanders 1998, Aaltonen et al. 2004).

Of the many arising insights perhaps none was more surprising or useful to researchers than the finding that complex systems across the board share a significant number of the following characteristics. (Ilachinski 2004, Ilachinski 2006, CSCS). When used together they provide a set of insights and questions that form the framework for a new understanding of how the future emerges:

1. Diversity among the components – heterogeneous parts or 'agents' – is a source of novelty in the system and ensures ongoing evolution, regeneration and adaptation;

2. Non-linear interactions, such as; widespread information flow and feedback loops;

3. Self-organization; which results from attractors in the system, and which form adaptations in the larger environment and other agents;

4. Local information processing; which is local interaction among autonomous agents. Typically agents 'see' only their part of the system and act locally; no global control;

5. Emergence; exhibits unpredictable global behaviour or patterns; although spontaneous order emerges from local system interactions;

6. Adaptation is; open and responsive to changes in to the larger environment or context and to other agents in the system; continuously processing, learning and incorporating new information; making boundaries hard to define;

7. Organization across multiple scales; shows agents in the system organized into groups or hierarchies of some sort, which influence how the system evolves over time;

8. Sensitiveness to changes in initial conditions is about how small changes can create major effects at some point in the future;

9. Non-equilibrium; most interesting behaviour/creativity found at the 'edge of chaos'; healthy systems operate in a dynamic state somewhere between the

extremes of order and disorder, making it easier for them to adapt to changing conditions;

10. Best understood by observing the behaviour, i.e. activities, processes, adaptation of the whole system over time; refers to qualitative descriptions and understanding when compared to quantitative descriptions.

The Emergence of the Future

These insights provide us with a promising new way to explore the question 'What is the future?' They also provide new ways to describe how the future arises, evolves and is influenced.

In classic deterministic forecasting models, the future is merely an extension of existing conditions and trends. Classical forecasting models are based on the old cause and effect belief that given a set of present conditions all you have to do is project those forward and with a few twists and turns arrive at a conclusion about the future. However, forecasting based on the techniques of linear extrapolation has generated many famously inaccurate predictions about the future.

In contrast, one of the things that the complexity science tells us is that the behaviour of a complex system cannot be predicted from one's knowledge of the parts of the system.

Because the variables in a complex system interact constantly and change in response to each other and the larger environment, the system is non-linear. Therefore explanations about the future and methodologies for eliciting information about the future must incorporate our new understanding about system′s non-linear interactions.

Complex systems often surprise us, because through the process of emergence, a system as a whole creates new macro behaviour or new patterns of interaction – the future. Emergence refers to properties or a higher level of pattern created by the interactions of local agents in the system. (Johnson 2001, Ilachinski 2004). As a simple example of emergence, a computer programme developed by Craig Reynolds in 1986 and known as 'Boids' simulates the flocking behaviour of birds by programming the individual agents or boids to follow three simple rules: 1) maintain a minimum distance from other boids; 2) match the velocity of nearby boids; and 3) move toward the perceived centre of nearly boids. What appears to be very complex emergent behaviour arises from a set of fairly simple underlying rules.

No central boid directs this process. The boids, acting only on local information gathered from their immediate neighbours and their environment, create the dynamic elegant flocking patterns that are entirely unexpected; they cannot be predicted by just knowing the local rules defining what each boid does. Local simple rules create complex self-organizing global or macro behaviour. (Ilachinski 2004).

If we think of the future as new macro patterns of behaviour arising from the non-linear interactions of complex systems, then the future emerges primarily in two ways: 1) through a system's sensitiveness to new initial conditions and 2) through the process of adaptation.

Sensitiveness to Initial Conditions

In non-linear systems, a small change in one variable can spark changes in another and another. Non-linear, dynamic systems teem with creative potential and sensitiveness to new influences. This sensitiveness to new influences means that change can be introduced at almost any point. In non-linear systems, small changes or inputs of resources at strategic influence points can, if the system is sensitive to the change, propagate in space and time to bring about significant shifts in the overall system. (Lorenz 1963, Sanders 1998). A simple way to comprehend this is to imagine how a change in choices or decisions at certain points would lead a project, process or organization into different histories and different futures. (Nicolis and Prigogine 1989).

Here we try to pinpoint what we actually mean by sensitiveness to initial conditions, via a metaphor, a simulation, a visualisation and a story.

The Butterfly Effect 'a butterfly flapping its wings in Asia and causing a hurricane in the Atlantic' provided a beautiful metaphor for how small changes or events create complex results. It increased our understanding of how small systems interact with large systems; how a small change in the initial conditions multiplies upward, expanding into larger systems, changing conditions along the way. An increased understanding is that every time a new building block (e.g. the transistor, the Internet, Java programming language...) is presented to a system, a multiple number of changes start to occur. In his weather model meteorologist Edward Lorenz rounded one variable from 0,506127 to 0,506. The slight difference was enough to create a thunderstorm instead of sun; and to encourage Lorenz to develop his theory, which provided a new level of understanding about the chaotic behaviour of nonlinear systems (Lorenz 1993, Holland 1998).

The simple image that derived from the use of Jules-Henri Poincaré's phase space, translating numbers into shapes, which resembled the wings of butterfly or an owl's mask, is today known as the Lorenz Attractor. For the first time, it was possible to see the order hidden within the behaviour of a non-linear system. Three conclusions followed 1) there is order hidden beneath disorder that becomes visible when the behaviour of a system is seen as a whole, 2) patterns arise when the actors in a system are attracted to and interact with each others, and the attractions will create the boundaries of the pattern that in turn will create the internal design of the system, 3) the prediction of non-linear systems remains impossible, but it may be possible to provide better qualitative descriptions of a system's characteristics and behaviour as a whole over time. (Sanders 1998).

The discovery was contradictory to how we have been taught to think, i.e. our success depends on the carefully laid out plans and visions we make, and the skill and devotion we used to execute them. We have been trained to design and manage the change. If we look back at OD projects in recent years, we notice that a lot of effort has been focused on managing internal change processes to make people and organizations more competitive, but less to shape the strategic context within which we work. In brief, we tend to decide to do something different, to re-structure or to re-engineer, and then develop a plan to carry it out.

The classic sand pile simulation serves as another illustration of how small systems interact with large systems.

> An observer who studies a specific area of a pile can easily identify the mechanisms that cause sand to fall, and he or she can even predict whether avalanches will occur in the near future. To a local observer, large avalanches would remain unpredictable, however, because they are a consequence of the total history of the entire pile. The criticality is a global property of the sand pile. (Bak and Chen, 1991).

The starting point for the physicists Per Bak and Kan Chen (ibid.) was their dissatisfaction with the main stream tradition that was used to analyse large interactive systems; they were analysed in the same way as the small, orderly systems had been analysed. The belief that the behaviour of a large interactive system could be predicted by studying its elements separately and analysing mechanisms individually was challenged by self-organized criticality theory. It suggests a different approach, which can be stated as: many composite systems naturally evolve towards a critical state where a minor event can start a chain reaction that can affect any number of elements in the system. Furthermore, composite systems never reach equilibrium but move from one metastable state to the next.

Even a small change introduces plurality, and because of the systems' dynamics and the excessive number of direct and indirect feedback loops the results are new, and non-linear. Therefore linear presentations of the future, extrapolations and business-as-usual scenarios, can be helpful, but in limited, stable circumstances. In chaotic systems a small initial uncertainty grows over time. As one attempts to make predictions further into the future, the amount of information one needs to gather about the initial conditions increases exponentially over time and long-term predictions become extremely difficult. Consequently we focus on identifying and influencing the future as it is emerging.

In addition to the above, complex systems consist of many agents that act in parallel, they typically have many niches, which can be exploited by an agent able to anticipate a possibility and adapt to fill it. And filling the niches creates new niches – new opportunities are always being created in complex systems as long as the system does not reach equilibrium. (Waldrop, 1992; Kauffman, 2000; Mitleton-Kelly, 2003). This results in increased complexity, and the more complex a system, the more states and properties it can manifest, and furthermore, novel features create interlevel causal relationships and higher levels of organization that did not previously exist. (C.f. Juarrero, 1999).

After an enlightening metaphor and a ground-breaking simulation we would like present sensitiveness to initial conditions in a graphic form. The baker's transformation serves us for that purpose. Imagine a baker rolling out a ball of pastry dough. He takes some dough, works it into a sheet with a rolling pin, folds it over itself a few times, and then rolls it out again. Now, let us place two dots on the pastry sheet and see how the two spots, originally close to each other get pushed apart in the baker's transformation. The two operations, stretching the dough by rolling it out and folding it back again, can be stated in mathematical terms.

> The stretching corresponds to a locally unstable equilibrium, one from which all nearby points is repelled, because when we stretch the dough each point is moved away from all its neighbours. The folding operation is the mathematical counterpart of a system whose space is bounded so that the space cannot be stretched everywhere. (Casti 2000, 71).

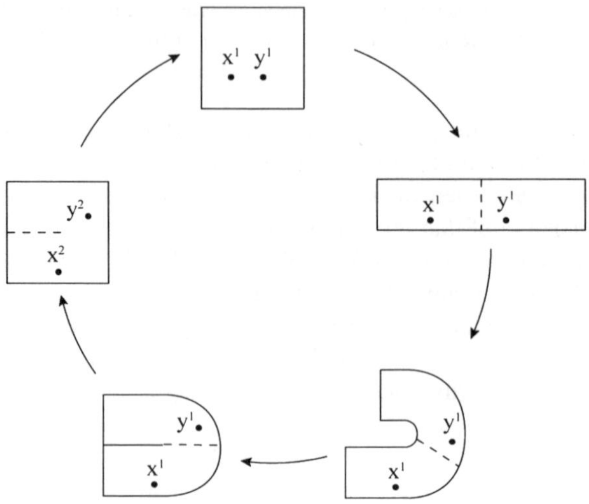

Figure 7.1 Baker's transformation

As a concluding example of sensitiveness to initial conditions we recall the story of the largest blackout in United States on 14 August 2003. On that day twenty percent of the North American power grid, including parts of the Midwest and most of the North-Eastern United States and Ontario, Canada, went down. This enormous power outage was the result of many interacting and interdependent smaller events that kept over fifty million people in the dark for hours. (Iwata 2003).

In addition to disrupting business, industry and government, the power outage disrupted water, transportation, and communication services, and resulted in an estimated six billion dollars of outage-resulted financial losses. And the fact that it did not spread further, because engineers in Valley Forge, Pennsylvania were able to isolate other parts of the system from the cascading collapse, raises some interesting questions about the vulnerabilities of interdependent systems, including the rapidly globalizing world economy. (Sanders and McCabe 2003).

Embracing Discontinuity and Asymmetry

If we agree that non-linear dynamics applies to most of our social world, then the old enemies of strategic thinkers, discontinuity and asymmetry, are not necessarily our enemies anymore, instead they can turn into our allies in the emergence of the future.

The French marketing expert Jean-Marie Dru (1996) flagged for disruption long before the masses addressed their attention to it. For him discontinuity is a source of progress, and understanding it is in the core of disruption.

> Disruption is about finding the strategic idea that breaks and overturns a convention in the marketplace, and then makes it possible to reach a new vision or to give new substance to an existing vision. (ibid. 54).

Disruption creates new initial conditions. It starts from hindsight, from identifying the existing conventions in your strategic landscape, in your market place, in your business. Then it searches out reference points for discontinuities and asymmetries. They can be found inside the organization through a thorough rethinking process that leads to the reframing of its activities; or they can be found outside the organization, when an organization re-examines itself taking into account the changing marketplace. And finally, it replaces the existing convention with a new vision that aims at creating a new convention. Without a replacing vision we have only a short interruption, a small disturbance to the linear development.

Discontinuities and asymmetries are signs of opportunities. We seek to benefit from them by using sensitiveness to initial conditions as a conceptual tool. Let us take two examples: a poet and a physicist at their daily work. While they both strive to go beneath the surface of events, the poet concentrates on the human condition, the physicist on the material side. For a poet, a broken rhyme invokes close attention and the possibility for new interpretation. For a physicist, a lack of symmetry suggests the existence of new particles. The poet relies on the interplay between the denotative and connotative levels of language to create meaning not obvious on the surface. The physicist has to count on the conventions made in mathematics and physics to make his observations valid to the scientific audience. (C.f. Holland 1998).

For Clayton Christensen (Cristensen et al. 2004) disruption is a strategy that creates and capitalises on asymmetries. He recognizes two major types of asymmetries: 1) asymmetric motivation, and 2) asymmetric skills. The former has a lot to do with the respective perspectives the opportunities are viewed from, a tempting opportunity for one organization is not necessarily tempting to another. The latter refers simply to the capabilities to do something.

Disruptive entrants can either increase access and ability to a product or service that was earlier beyond the possibilities of many people or they can help customers do more easily and effectively what they were already doing. In both cases entrants take advantage of asymmetries that are on their side. They could be new benefits like convenience, customization, or coolness. Consequently, in disrupting circumstances new entrants will bypass existing skills, processes and resources in the markets.

The most common type of asymmetry however is asymmetric information. It is a key concept in game theory, agency theory, transaction costs economics and theories of property rights; and the relationship between asymmetric information and innovation has been explored e.g. in investment strategies, patent races and patent licensing. (Beggs 1992, Alexandrou and Sudarsanam 2001, Albano 2001, Davis 2001).

Asymmetric information may arise inside organizations (between divisions, units, teams, people) and between them (buyers, suppliers, competitors etc.). Either way there are differences in the types of information held by the actors; the information can be available, but it may be unevenly distributed, and the differences in the information sets held by actors are unobservable. It is suggested that an organizations' success does not depend solely on their quality to develop new products and processes but in addition on their ability to exploit information asymmetries. This is because the information generated in organizations' various activities is initially private and not available to others. (C.f. Davis 2001).

Steven Metz and Douglas V. Johnson II (2001, 5) define asymmetry as 'acting, organizing, and thinking differently than one´s opponents in order to maximise one's own advantages, exploit an opponent's weaknesses, attain an initiative, or gain greater freedom of action.'

The guiding idea is that there exist significant differences of some kind, and that these can be identified and exploited. Consequently, we should have an idea, or elaborated ideas, where significant differences could be found. The sources for them are many, besides asymmetric information, skills and motivation they can derive from methods, concepts and frameworks used in organizations' strategic work as well as from ways of organizing and using technologies; and from the belief and value systems, or the conceptions of time that organizations embody. Thus, they derive from differences in the most grounded practices of organizational life – the ways organizations make sense of their worlds.

Identifying and Influencing Coming Changes

We suggest that instead of reducing ambiguity in organizations' strategic work it might be more pertinent to assess those issues that are not under our control – not the symmetry, but the asymmetry, not the continuity, but the discontinuity – in order to improve the quality of our sense-making and decision-making.

We do not live in static world, the social systems which most of our daily lives take place in, are non-linear dynamic systems full of connections, relationships and changes. Moreover social systems are capable of processing and incorporating new information and as a result of that they keep changing.

In organizations change occurs as a system creates and responds to changes in itself through a process of feedback. A new pattern emerges when information on issues, trends and technologies flows and people and organizations interact and converge through actions taken by them. An innovation of one organization forces action by others, and results in a feedback loop to which they all are sensitive. (See Sanders 1998).

More than imagining and presenting the future as an extrapolation of the present, we look for approaches that allow us to see and influence the future by responding to and influencing what is emerging. In this work, the ability to think non-linearly is critical, as are the abilities to make sense of asymmetries and exploit them advantageously. We assume that there exists a relationship between order and disorder and that change occurs as a result of their interaction and as new influences disrupt existing patterns of working, organizing and interacting. Out of these disruptions, and as we move towards new attractors, new patterns are formed.

We suggest that sensitiveness to initial conditions could be the theory-constitutive metaphor that would permit us to rethink the underlying logic of change and to reconceptualise cause. This is a promise founded on the possibility of incorporating emergence into our sense-making and decision-making processes. (Aaltonen 2005).

Table 7.1 Approaches for identifying and influencing sensitiveness to initial conditions

Identifying	Influencing
Multiple perspectives	Reframing
Difference questioning	Setting or removing constraints
Network analysis	Coupling
Computing	Adding or removing 'noise'
Pattern management	Attractors
Language games	Engagement of minds and hearts
Visual modelling	Perception management

The approaches are thematic entities that can entail a number of more detailed methods. They can be used alone or in combination with others. An insightful combination of various, even contradictory approaches can create foresight. Sometimes the difference between identifying and influencing your systems' new initial conditions is only semantic; as identifying already includes influencing or noting that one is not able to influence them without first identifying them. At other times identifying precedes responding; you first need to make sense of the coming changes then you prepare yourself to face them.

On the left side of table 7.1, we have placed the thematic entities that are used in identifying new initial conditions. They are context-sensitive, their successful use requires the ability to assess the situation and select appropriate approaches. Multiple perspectives are needed to see emerging conditions, scanning across industries and disciplines, and generally the use of complementary and contradictory information sources helps us to notice differences and point to new opportunities. Network analysis can reveal the hidden logic of connections and relationship, simulations can be helpful in probing and representing system dynamics, and pattern management to find out what drives the emergent patterns of behaviour. The skilful use of language and visual modelling are necessary approaches to make sense of a large amount of information, to lift it up to a higher conceptual level and to create meaning and action from it.

The right side of table 7.1 presents approaches for influencing and managing the context an organization operates within and it is consciously targeted at the creation of and benefiting from new initial conditions. Furthermore, by reframing attacks at a conceptual level on the existing conventions or boundaries in the system and by disrupting them a new space of opportunities opens. The introduction of new attractors energizes the system and shifts it to a new state, which can be further monitored and beneficial attractors can be stabilised. By coupling certain elements together we influence their emergence, as we do by setting or removing constraints by making different types of resources available to a system and by injecting or removing certain kinds of information, 'noise', from a system, and by manipulating perceptions. Also, the psychological dimensions of the media and the conduits used to influence people's minds and hearts is another powerful source of change.

Conclusions

In our interconnected world, with instant access to news and information, it is important to recognise that new initial conditions often take the form of ideas, media reports, economic and market conditions, as well as political and cultural conflicts. It is very hard if not impossible to see all the new initial conditions since they are constantly being created. But, understanding this concept and using tools that incorporate this idea are very important when thinking about how the future emerges and how it is possible to influence the evolution of the future.

In addition to change initiated by sensitiveness to initial conditions, system change also occurs through the process of adaptation. Systems are influenced and shaped by changes in the larger context or environment in which they operate. In order to survive, the system as a whole must adapt to changes in the larger environment be they new traffic patterns, new economic or political conditions or new technologies.

To benefit from these insights, we must take into consideration the fact that social systems are historically emerging and socially constructed. People and organizations are aware of themselves as historical beings. In this way they are reflexive with regard to their histories, where they come from and what they were yesterday, and their futures that are constrained and enabled by their histories. People and organizations are actively involved in the co-creation of social reality, and as a result social systems are both the medium and outcome of these participatory processes. (C.f. Introna 2003).

We have sketched an approach that is perhaps less effective for improving the existing practices but more suited to shaping the strategic context as it is emerging and benefiting from the changes that are occurring within it.

Chapter 8

Making Sense of a Complex World

Paul Cilliers

Introduction

The issues around knowledge – *what* can we know about the world, *how* do we know it, what is the *status* of our experiences – have been central to philosophical reflection for ages. Answers to these questions, admittedly oversimplified here, have traditionally taken one of two forms. On the one hand there is the belief that the world can be made rationally transparent, that with enough hard work, knowledge about the world can be made objective. Thinkers like Descartes and Habermas are often framed as being responsible for this kind of attitude. It goes under numerous names including positivism, modernism, objectivism, rationalism and epistemological fundamentalism. On the other hand, there is the belief that knowledge is only possible from a personal or cultural-specific perspective, and that it can therefore never be objective or universal. This position is ascribed, correctly or not, to numerous thinkers in the more recent past like Kuhn, Rorty and Derrida, and its many names include relativism, idealism, post-modernism, perspectivism and flapdoodle.

Relativism is not a position that can be maintained consistently, and of course the thinkers mentioned above have far more sophisticated positions than portrayed in this bipolar caricature.[1] There are also recent thinkers who attempt to move beyond the fundamentalist/relativist dichotomy, as we will try to do here, but it seems to me that when it comes to the technological applications of theories of knowledge, there is an implicit reversion to one of these traditional positions. For those who want to computerize knowledge, knowledge has to be objective. It must be possible to gather, store and manipulate knowledge without the intervention of a subject. The critics of formalized knowledge, on the other hand, usually fall back on arguments based on subjective or culture-specific perspectives to show that it is not possible, that we cannot talk about knowledge independently of the knowing subject.

1 If relativism is maintained consistently, it becomes an absolute position. From this one can see that a relativist is nothing else but a disappointed fundamentalist. However, this should not lead one to conclude that everything that is *called* post-modern leads to this weak position. Lyotard's seminal work, *The Postmodern Condition* (Lyotard 1984.), is subtitled *A Report on Knowledge*. He is primarily concerned with the structure and form of different kinds of knowledge, not with relativism. An informed reading of Derrida will also show that deconstruction does not imply relativism at all (see Cilliers 2005). For a penetrating philosophical study of the problem, see *Against Relativism* (Norris 1997).

I am of the opinion that a shouting match between these two positions will not get us much further. The first thing we have to do is to acknowledge the complexity of the problem we are dealing with. This will unfortunately not lead us out of the woods, but it should enable a discussion that is more fruitful than the objectivist/subjectivist debate. In what follows the problem of making sense of the world will be examined from the perspective of complexity theory. Complexity will be introduced briefly, followed by a discussion of why it is so difficult to have knowledge of complex things. We generate understanding through the making of models, and therefore the modelling of complexity is a central issue. The problem of modelling will be discussed with reference to the role played by causation, with specific attention paid to the notion of circularity. Finally, the implications of this argument will be discussed with reference to the inevitability of normative and ethical considerations when we deal with a complex world.

What Is Complexity?

There are different understandings of complexity theory and its implications. On the one hand, there is a more strictly mathematical and computational view. This view is often developed via insights from chaos theory. In the cases where such a 'hard' understanding is uncritically appropriated by the human sciences, it can lead to exactly the kind of positivism which is being argued against in this paper. On the other hand, there is a more critical understanding of complexity. This view argues that complexity theory does not provide us with exact tools to solve our complex problems, but shows us (in a rigorous way) exactly why these problems are so difficult.[2] This second view may have a more skeptical perspective on what can be done with complexity theory, but it is developed from an understanding that is not really at odds with a generally accepted scientific characterisation of complexity. These characteristics can be summarized in the following way:[3]

1. Complex systems are open systems. Since they interact with their environments, the *context* in which a certain system operates is as important as the characteristics of the system itself. Thus there are always contingent issues to take into consideration;

2. They operate under conditions not at equilibrium;

3. Complex systems consist of many components. The components themselves are often simple (or can be treated as such);

4. The output of components is a function of their inputs. At least some of these

2 See Richardson and Cilliers (2001) for a discussion of some of these issues.

3 These characteristics were formulated in collaboration with Fred Boogerd and Frank Bruggemans at the department of Molecular Cell Physiology at the Free University, Amsterdam. Similar lists by Holland (1998: 225 - 231), Emmeche (1997) Kauffman (1971) and Cilliers (1998) were consulted in the process.

functions must be non-linear;

5. The state of the system is determined by the values of the inputs and outputs;

6. Interactions are defined by actual input-output relationships and they are dynamic (the strength of the interactions change over time);

7. Components on average interact with many others. There are often multiple routes possible between components, mediated in different ways;

8. Some sequences of interaction will provide feedback routes, whether long or short;

9. Complex systems display behaviour that results from the *interaction* between components and not from characteristics inherent to the components themselves. This is sometimes called emergence;

10. Asymmetrical structure (temporal, spatial and functional organization) is developed, maintained and adapted in complex systems through internal dynamic processes. Structure is maintained even though the components themselves are exchanged or renewed;

11. Complex systems display behaviour over a divergent range of timescales. This is necessary in order for the system to cope with its environment. It must adapt to changes in the environment quickly, but it can only sustain itself if at least part of the system changes at a slower rate than changes in the environment[4]. This part can be seen as the 'memory' of the system;

12. The behaviour and characteristics of complex systems unfold in time. The history of the system co-determines the current behaviour of the system. The importance of temporal aspects of complexity is often underestimated;

13. More than one description of a complex system is possible. Different descriptions will decompose the system in different ways. Different descriptions may also have different degrees of complexity.

If one considers the implications of these characteristics carefully a number of insights and problems arise:

1. The *structure* of a complex system enables it to behave in complex ways. If there is too little structure, for example many degrees of freedom, the system can behave more randomly, but not more functionally. The mere 'capacity' of the system (for example the total amount of degrees of freedom available if the system was not structured in any way) does not serve as a meaningful indicator of the complexity of the system. Complex behaviour is possible

---

4 Issues around slowness, appropriate speed and the temporal nature of complex systems in general are discussed in Cilliers (2006).

when the behaviour of the system is constrained. On the other hand, a fully constrained system has no capacity for complex behaviour either. This claim is not quite the same as saying that complexity exists somewhere on the edge between order and chaos. A wide range of structured systems display complex behaviour. In general it is useful to think of complex systems in terms of a network of interactions. The structure of the system is defined by the strengths of the various connections in the network. Some of these connections may be fixed and/or pre-determined; others can change over time;

2. Since different descriptions of a complex system decompose the system in different ways, the knowledge gained by any description is always relative to the perspective from which the description was made. This does not imply that any description is as good as any other. It is merely the result of the fact that only a limited number of characteristics of the system can be taken into account by any specific description. Although there is no *a priori* procedure for deciding which description is correct, some descriptions will deliver more interesting results than others;

3. In describing the macro-behaviour (or emergent behaviour) of the system, not all the micro-features can be taken into account. The description is a reduction of complexity. Nevertheless, macro-behaviour is not the result of anything else but the micro-activities of the system. Yet, to describe the macro-behaviour purely in terms of the micro-features is a difficult task. When we do science, we usually work with descriptions which operate mainly on a macro-level, but these descriptions will, more often than not, be approximations of some kind;

4. Activity on the macro level can also influence activity on the micro-level. In a way the notion of 'level' is problematic here since the system and all its components exist in a contingent reality. 'Levels' are usually a result of our *description* of the system, rather than an inherent ontological feature of the system itself. We will return to this issue when we deal with causality.

These insights have important implications for the knowledge-claims we make when dealing with complex systems[5]. To *fully* understand a complex system, we need to understand it in all its complexity. Furthermore, because complex systems are open systems, we need to understand the system's complete environment before we can understand the system. Moreover, the environment is complex in itself. There is no human way of doing this. The knowledge we have of complex systems is based on the models we make of these systems, but in order to function as models – and not merely as a repetition of the system – they have to *reduce* the complexity of the system. This means that some aspects of the system are always left out of consideration. The problem is compounded by the fact that that which is left out,

5 The notion 'complex system' is used in a generalised way to refer any system which is constituted through complex non-linear interactions. Examples would include living systems, social systems, economic systems, organizations, language, eco-systems etc.

interacts with the rest of the system in a non-linear way and we can therefore not predict what the effects of our reduction of the complexity will be, especially not as the system and its environment develops and transforms in time.

We cannot have complete knowledge of complex systems; we can only have knowledge in terms of a certain framework. There is no stepping outside of complexity (we are finite beings), thus there is no framework for frameworks. We *choose* our frameworks. This choice need not be arbitrary in any way, but it does mean that the status of the framework (and the framework itself) will have to be continually revised. Our knowledge of complex systems is always provisional[6]. We have to be modest about the claims we make about such knowledge. The issues around knowledge, understanding and modelling need to be elaborated a little further.

Complexity and Understanding

An understanding of knowledge as constituted within a complex system of interactions would, on the one hand, deny that knowledge can be seen as atomised 'facts' that have objective meaning. Knowledge comes to be in a dynamic network of interactions, a network that does not have distinctive borders. On the other hand, this perspective would also deny that knowledge is something purely subjective, mainly because one cannot conceive of the subject as something *prior* to the 'network of knowledge', but rather as something constituted *within* that network. The argument from complexity thus wants to move beyond the objective/subjective dichotomy. The dialectical relationship between knowledge and the system within which it is constituted has to be acknowledged. The two do not exist independently, thus making it impossible to first sort out the system (or context), and then to identify the knowledge within the system. This co-determination also means that knowledge and the system within which it is constituted is in constant transformation. What appears to be uncontroversial at one point may not remain so for long.

The points made above are just a restatement of the claim that complex systems have a history, and that they cannot be conceived of without taking their context into account. The burning question at this stage is whether it is possible to *do* that formally or computationally. Can we incorporate the context and the history of a system into its description, thereby making it possible to extract knowledge from it? This is certainly possible (and very useful) in the case of relatively simple systems, but with complex systems there are a number of problems. These problems are, at least to my mind, not of a metaphysical, but of a practical nature.

The issue is complicated by two factors: the non-linear nature of complexity and the fact that it is often extremely difficult to decide what part of the system is and what is part of its environment. There is no meta-position from which we can 'frame' the system. We will return to these two issues below, but for now we can state that the way in which we approach our understanding is the result of a certain strategy, not an objective quest for absolute knowledge.

---

6 For a similar view, see Najmanovich (2002).

The problematic nature of our understanding of complexity should become clear now. We do not have the means to understand complex systems in their complexity. There are always factors we did not or could not take into consideration and we have no way of knowing what the effects of that will be. Does this imply that our knowledge of the world is arbitrary, that the sense we make is purely constructed? I do not think so, but in order to answer this question better, we have to pay close attention to how we model complex systems.

Models

The notion of a model is central to all forms of understanding. The notion will be used here in a wide sense (for example theories and systems of rules can also be seen as models). In the context of complexity, the role of models is described in the following way by Csányi (in Khalil and Boulding 1996: 148):

> Any kind of scientific statement, concept, law, and any description of a phenomenon is a model construction which tries to reflect phenomena of the external world. Reality is extremely complex; it consists of strongly or more weakly related events. Science makes an attempt to separate and isolate different effects and phenomena. It seeks the simplest relationships by which examined phenomena can at least be described or demonstrated. It creates simplified models which only partly reflect reality, but which allow contemplation, and what is most important, pragmatic, even if sometimes modest, predictions.

We cannot deal with reality in all its complexity. Our models *have* to reduce this complexity in order to generate some understanding. In the process something is obviously lost. If we have a good model, we would hope that which is left out is unimportant. It should be clear already that purely quantitative models of complex systems, which abstract from a set of real properties to numerical values, will be problematic (Emetine 1997, 54). The underlying problem with models of complexity is, however, even more serious. No matter how we construct the model, it will be flawed, and what is more, we do not know in which way it is flawed.

In order to understand this claim we have to remember the non-linear nature of the interactions in complex systems. This non-linearity has two important consequences. In the first place, when there are a lot of simultaneous, non-linear interactions, it soon becomes impossible to keep track of causal relationships between components. Secondly, from the non-linear nature of complex systems we can deduce that they are incompressible (Cilliers 1998, 10). What is more, they change with time. The problem is a difficult one: Models have to reduce the complexity of the phenomena being described; they have to leave something out. However, we have no way of predicting the importance of that which is not considered. In a non-linear world where we cannot track a clear causal chain, something that may appear to be unimportant now, may turn out to be vitally important later. Or *vice versa*, of course. Our models have to 'frame' the problem in a certain way, and this framing will inevitably introduce distortions.

This is not an argument against the construction of models. We have no choice but to make models if we want to understand the world. It is just an argument that models of complex systems will always be flawed in principle, and that we have to acknowledge these limitations.

What then of the argument that it may be possible to incorporate absolutely all the information concerning a complex system into some fancy (neural network or genetic algorithm) model? I do not wish to argue that it is impossible to repeat the complexity of a system in another medium, but one should remember that we now have a 'model' that is as complex as the system being modelled. It will be as difficult to understand as the system itself, and its behaviour will be as unpredictable. If the history of the model and the history of the system is not kept identical (and I cannot see how this can be done in anything but the most trivial of cases), the two will soon become uncorrelated. We have to conclude that it is impossible to have a perfect model of a complex system. This is not because of some inadequacy in our modelling techniques, but a result of the meaning of the notions 'model' and 'complex'. There will always be a gap between the two. This gap should serve as a creative impulse that continually challenges us to transform our models, not as a reason to give up.

The claim that our models of complex systems cannot be perfect introduces a next layer of problems: what is it then that is described by our models? Are they merely constructions or instruments, or do they reflect reality in some way? Both claims have had strong support. One way of naming these two traditions is to say that the attempt to reflect nature (accurately) is a modern approach, and that giving up that attempt is post-modern. Emmeche (1997, 54) argues that we can only deal with complexity if we adopt elements from both kinds of ethos. One can make a slightly stronger and more difficult demand: both approaches should be followed simultaneously. We are always busy with the world itself, and simultaneously, we cannot grasp it fully. Let us explore this a little further.

A distinction is often made between 'descriptive' or 'epistemological' complexity and 'ontological' complexity (for example by McIntyre 1998). The first has to do with the complexity of our descriptions, the second with the 'actual' complexity of things in the world. If one maintains this distinction, it would be easy to fall into the kind of dichotomy mentioned above. We would have descriptions of the world, and separate from it, the world itself. This is the trap stepped into by the classical approach to artificial intelligence: trying to make formal models that should represent the world accurately (see Colliers 1998, 58–88). The relationship between our descriptions of the world and the world itself is, however, more complex. There is a constant to and fro between them in which our models and, especially in the case of the human sciences, the world itself is transformed. Since our models cannot 'fit' the world exactly, there are many degrees of freedom in which they can move. They are, however, simultaneously constrained by the world in many ways. There is feedback from the world that tells us something about the appropriateness of our models. The situation is the following: there is, on the one hand, considerable freedom in modelling, but there are also, on the other hand, constraints from reality. The two are not independent of each other.

It is important to realise that the notion of a constraint is not a negative one. It is not something which merely limits possibilities, constraints are also *enabling*. By eliminating certain possibilities, others are introduced. Constraints provide a framework that enables descriptions to be built up around it[7]. When dealing with complexity, though, these frameworks cannot be fixed. They are constantly being transformed, and therefore our models will always be provisional.

What then is it that is described by our models? I would argue that models attempt to grasp the *structure* of complex systems. Complex systems are neither homogenous, nor chaotic. They have structure, embodied in the patterns of interactions between the components[8]. Some of these structures can be stable and long lived (and are therefore easier to catch in or models), whilst others can be volatile and ephemeral. These structures are also intertwined in a complex way. We find structure on all scales[9]. It is difficult to capture or grasp these structures, but since structure is constitutive of the nature of complex systems, there is something which provides a sounding board for the process of modelling and making sense. The sounding board is in itself a dynamic thing, but it allows us to make some claims which are not arbitrary.

Part of the reason for this is that we have not given up on the notion of causality completely. Although we cannot maintain a classical notion of causality, complexity is not random, chaotic or the result of pure chance. Let us briefly examine the role of causality in complex systems.

Complexity and Causality

Many thinkers have grappled with the problem of how to understand causality. Aristotle, one of the most influential, argued that we should not think of causality as a single, unified concept. He therefore distinguished four forms of causality: material, formal, efficient and final. With the decline of Aristotelian cosmology after the Enlightenment, and the resistance to teleological thinking in general after Darwin, his theory of causality also fell into disrepute. His position has received renewed attention with the rise of complexity thinking, specifically because it does not assume a simple linear relationship between cause and effect.[10]

Another very influential position on causality was developed by Hume. He argued that events are loose and separate, that there is no 'causal nexus' which ties cause and effect together. We cannot track the causal chain from cause to effect because

---

7 For a more detailed discussion of constraints, see Juarrero (1999, 131–150) and Cilliers (2001).

8 The notion of 'structure' is used in many different and confusing ways. In this analysis it refers to the patterns of interaction in the system, and underplays a distinction between the structure on the one hand, and activities within that structure on the other. Structure is the *result* of action in the system, not something that has to exist in an *a priori* fashion. The advantages of a network model of complexity is that we can depict rather stable structures, as well as more volatile ones using the same means (see Cilliers 1998, 99–100).

9 Structure is not chaotic, but may have a fractal nature (Csányi in Khalil and Boulding 1996, 158), especially if the system is critically organized (see Cilliers 1998, 96–98).

10 It will not receive further attention here. See Juarrero (1999) and Rosen (1991).

we cannot identify the mechanism by which the one is transformed into the other. Thus the notion of causality itself is somewhat empty. At best we can talk about the contiguity of events; we have to be careful when trying to relate them more tightly.

Directly or indirectly, this skeptical position has had a big influence on the understanding of causality in complexity thinking. Since the relationship between cause and effect is non-linear – small causes can have large effect, and vice versa – the tendency has been to give up the notion of causality. The metaphor of the so-called 'butterfly effect' used to explain non-linearity – that a butterfly flapping its wings in the Amazon can cause a hurricane in Indonesia – is a telling example. There is no reasonable meaning to the word 'cause' in this example. Millions of butterflies are flapping their wings all the time to no significant effect.

To the extent that this line of thinking, prevalent in complexity thinking inspired by chaos theory, sensitises us to the problematic nature of causality in complex systems, it is useful. However, I would argue that it causes more damage than the insight is worth. Most people who hear this example will not realise that it deconstructs itself. The idea of a traditional relationship between a single cause and a single effect will actually be reinforced. The point is that the hurricane is the result of a complex set of causes. To identify one of them on its own provides no real insight into the process. Causality itself must be understood as an interactive process.

The crux of the argument is the following: We cannot track a direct chain between cause and effect in a complex system. There are too many non-linear interactions involved. This, however, does not mean that we have to give up the notion of causality as such, as Hume would argue. The price for doing that is too high. Without any notion of causality it is difficult to see how one can assume any other position but a kind of constructive relativism. Events, even complex ones, do not happen at random just because we cannot *predict* them. The argument against determinism – a tricky one in itself – should not result in the dismissal of all forms of causality.

It is clear that we cannot rehabilitate a conventional linear understanding of causality in the form of a chain. A good point of departure would be to think of a complex system as a rich network of interactions with many loops and feedback routes. Causality is at work in all the minute little interactions on the micro-level in the system. The butterfly flapping its wings is not causing the hurricane, but it could be causing the butterfly to fly from flower A to flower B. This could result in flower B being pollinated, not flower A, given that a whole array of other causal and contingent relationships are also enacted. In a way one could say that there is nothing which determines the behaviour of a complex system but a lot of small causes interacting all the time. The problem is that we cannot track them all.

The problem is made explicit by conceptualising what is happening on the micro-level. Activity at a certain node in the network 'causes' a certain effect at the nodes to which it is connected. The 'effect' at each of these nodes is not only determined by this single 'cause' but by all the other 'causes' also influencing those nodes. Thus the effect of a certain cause is distributed over the network in a divergent way. Some aspect may be enhanced, others suppressed, by contingent conditions at various nodes. Moreover, since there are feedback paths, the effect of a certain cause can reflect back on itself. This can happen fairly directly, or after various lengths of mediated routes. In complex systems causes can thus affect themselves. Causality does not work in a linear chain, but in loops and circles.

This notion of circular causality can be expanded further. The activities on the micro-level give rise to behaviour we can identify on a larger scale or macro-level. The general term used for this phenomenon is 'emergence'. Consciousness is an emergent property of the brain (and the rest of the body), inflation is an emergent property of an economic system, and meaning is an emergent property of language. Emergent properties are not, however, merely *effects*, there is multi-way communication. Phenomena on the macro-level can affect activity on the micro-level. The idea of tasty food can lead to secretion of saliva, even if there is no food in the mouth (or within sight or smelling distance). Talk about inflation can influence the value of a currency, and lead to changes in inflation. Treating your employees as if they are stupid may actually turn them into stupid employees. Causality does not simply work from micro-causes to macro-effects. There is also a top-down process at work which means that causality in complex systems is circular.

Since the emergent properties of the system are 'caused' by the activity on the micro-level, and that micro-activities can be causally effected by macro-phenomena, the notion of level should be used with care here. It is an oversimplification to think of a system in terms of a level of material activity leading to a 'higher' level of epi-phenomena. There are various aggregates of nodes of different sizes operating in concert leading to an intricate mix of higher, lower and intermediate activities. The idea of a 'level' is rarely a natural characteristic of the system itself; it is more a function of the way in which we decompose the system.

If we take this characterization of causality in complex systems seriously, one can rightfully ask whether we have gained anything. By showing that causality is impossible to trace, are we not reduced to the same position as those who are sceptical about the very notion of causality? I think not, and there are two reasons.

The first reason is strategically important. The choice between thinking that causality does not really exist and thinking that it does exist, despite our inability to track it down accurately, has implications for how we conceive of a complex system in the first place. If we choose the first option, it is as if we have given up on understanding the system. All that we can really do is try some brute-force modelling system which bypasses our understanding, or just wave our hands. The second option is more difficult, but also more meaningful. The recognition that we cannot track down causality completely does not imply that we cannot look for causal patterns, even if these will have to be contextualized. We will only attempt the search for patterns, another name for sense-making, if we acknowledge some role for causality in the basic scheme of things.

The second reason has more pragmatic implications. Complex systems are not chaotic or random things. They have structure, and often much of this structure is quite robust. This means that some of the causal patterns may be quite persistent and thus something which can be both modelled and understood, albeit in a limited way. The argument presented here can be summarized, in the next section, by saying something about the sense we can make of complex systems without either claiming exact knowledge or throwing our hands in the air.

Bounded Understanding: Making Sense with Integrity

The fact that most of the things we have to deal with are complex makes it difficult to understand them. However, there is no easy way out. Understanding is generated in the confrontation with this difficulty. The argument is not that understanding is impossible, but that it is always constrained. Just as the characteristics of a complex system result from a certain structure which constrains the system, for example reduces the degrees of freedom, so our understanding of that system is also only possible within certain limits. There is no such thing as unconstrained understanding[11]. Knowing everything simultaneously destroys the ability to pick on what is relevant. A theory of everything is a theory of nothing specifically.

The question which remains is how do we play in this 'theatre of difficulty'? The discussion of complexity, models, structure and causality does not provide a final answer, but it does give us a number of important clues.

Primarily, it relieves us of the terrible duty to find the final, correct and objective description of the thing we are trying to understand. At the same time, it does not leave us with nothing to say, or with the idea that anything we say is as good as anything else. We are placed before a challenge to engage with that we wish to understand. There are a few things one can say about this engagement and the understanding which results. In conclusion I will look at four of them. It will be noticed that they all contain a certain circularity.

In the first place, understanding is always only possible within a certain context. Complex systems have intricate relationships with their environments in the sense that they are influenced by their environments but can also change it. This circularity is reflected in our understanding. We cannot make sense of a system in isolation, we have to take the context into consideration. The context, however, is not a given or static entity; it is in itself complex and changing. It is a mistake to think that we can somehow define or understand the context, and then use that to determine our understanding of the system. The circular relationship between system and environment means that our understanding has a dynamic nature, which leads us to the second important insight.

Our understanding of complex things is always provisional. Besides the constant interaction with its environment, parts of the internal structure of a complex system are always changing. Such systems have a memory which changes and grows, it can learn, it must adapt and it must anticipate the future. These are all dynamic non-linear processes. What may be a fairly accurate description at one stage may not remain so and therefore we have to review our understanding. Understanding something of a system already leads to a new understanding. This reflexive nature of our understanding is driven by a dynamic that is circular, but not in the sense of returning to itself or closing. There are always new things being circulated in the process.

The first two aspects, taken together, lead to a third: Our understanding of understanding complex things is not a passive activity. Just as a system is not a passive reflection of its environment, but also actively interpreting and transforming

11 See Cilliers (2001) for more detail.

it, so our understanding is not merely the result of absorbing information in a one way process. Two things happen in the process. In the first place, a certain description of a complex system may affect the system. This is especially true of complex social systems. Describing the system in a certain way leads to the system understanding itself differently, which leads to different and new characteristics and behaviour. In the second place, the subject doing the understanding is not merely passively receiving information; it is also being transformed by its own understanding. Some systems, like systems in nature, may be more self-contained than others, but in general one can say that at least in certain aspects, the system being described, and the one trying to understand the system, constitute each other in a circular way.

This insight leads directly to a fourth implication. Our descriptions of complex things are not neutral ones, developed from an objective position. Furthermore, we cannot describe them completely. We can only deal with complexity from a certain perspective; we have to leave things out. This involves choice. There is no position from which this choice can be determined accurately since that would imply a perfect meta-model of the system. Choice involves precisely that which we cannot calculate. Since choice is not based on calculation, it always involves a normative dimension. What does this mean? It means that when we are trying to understand complex things, we are not involved in a purely descriptive activity, but also in an ethical one[12].

It should be clear that 'ethical' is not used here as some substitute for the notion 'subjective' (as in 'my understanding is purely subjective'). It serves to indicate the limits of our understanding. This understanding is neither subjective, nor complete and objective. It is the result of a process of engagement which involves choice, and these choices co-determine the outcome of the process[13]. These choices have to be made explicit *as choices* in order to give meaning to the description. To offer descriptions of complex things *as if they were neutral* is unethical. Meaningful understanding of complex things has more to do with integrity than with objective accuracy.

In trying to make sense of the world we are neither lost in a mystical place, nor in a world of random or chance events. However, we are not operating in a perfectly ordered Legoland either. There are patterns to be discovered, but they are neither obvious nor permanent. In a way this is fortunate because it makes us human. If we lived in a mystical wood we would have been ephemeral. If we lived in a perfectly ordered world we would have been machines. Living in a complex world means that what we are and what we have to do have not been finalized yet. Making sense of the world is an adventure, not an algorithm.[14]

---

12 The relationships between ethics and complexity is discussed in more detail in Cilliers (2004)

13 See Rosen (1996) for a formal argument to this effect.

14 Parts of this chapter are based on material used in Cilliers (2000), (2001), and (2005).

Chapter 9

The Emergence of Final Cause

Eve Mitleton-Kelly

Introduction

Causality is a difficult concept, but one which needs to be considered carefully as it has significant practical applications in the sciences as well as in business. One of the earliest analyses of causality was by Aristotle, when he described four causes or four different aspects of cause as material, efficient, formal and final. During the seventeenth century *efficient* cause gained predominance, which led to much of science and economics adopting a mono-causal approach. In the last half century many scholars have began to re-examine the notion of causality. In the natural and social sciences, complexity theory has also contributed a fresh perspective. This chapter will explore that perspective and will attempt to link the Aristotelian concept to current discussions on causality in complexity theory.

Kaminska-Labbe et al (2006) show quite clearly that the recent legacy of *efficient* cause being the primary focus of science and economics is erroneous. They also show that *multiple causes co-evolve*. This chapter will build on that argument and suggest (a) that the notion of causality needs to be rethought as multiple non-linear[1] inter-related influences at different levels; (b) that vision and intention may contribute towards shaping or guiding final cause, but do not determine it, as the outcome is emergent; and (c) emergence needs to be thought of both as a top-down and a bottom-up reciprocal *process*, as well as an *outcome*.

The chapter will set the broad context by describing the four Aristotelian causes and the legacy of teleology, and describe some of the principles of complexity theory that have contributed to our richer understanding of multiple causality. The theory will be illustrated through practical examples to show how the emergent context created through interaction, constrains the behaviour of the participants. They in turn have to explore fresh alternatives and to create a new way of working, new relationships, and a different culture to achieve the intended final cause.

---

1 Non-linear generally refers to a situation that has a disproportionate cause and effect. A non-linear system is one whose behaviour is not simply the sum of its parts or their multiples. In complex systems there are often strong interactions between system parts and these interactions often lead to the emergence of patterns and cooperation. That is, they lead to structures that are the properties of groups of parts, and not of the individual constituents.

Many real-world problems appear intractable and are difficult to resolve. Part of the difficulty arises when only single causes are sought, when such problems arise from the interaction of multiple, underlying, and inter-related causes. Similarly when an example of 'good practice' is found, there is a mistaken assumption that simple copying of *what* was done and *how* it was done is adequate. But the results are often disappointing. Complexity theory would explain that, since the conditions are different when the 'best practice' is transferred, it is unlikely to work in the same way. A different approach would be to understand the multiple, underlying, inter-related principles (or causes) of *why* something worked well and what would have prevented it from working well. These underlying principles may then be used as insights to guide the adaptation of the successful experiment in a different context, by making it specific to the new organisational context.

The Complexity Group at the London School of Economics works with organisations that have apparently intractable problems and has developed a method based on complexity theory, of identifying the multiple, underlying causes that together create a problem or an enabling environment. The practical example that will be discussed in this chapter was part of a project which attempted to understand how one organization improved its alignment quite significantly. It will not offer any solutions, but it will illustrate some of the multiple, inter-related and co-evolving causes that together created an enabling environment which facilitated improved alignment. Making sense in an organization is part of understanding the full context in which decisions are made; while mono-causal approaches offer impaired sense-making and thus tend to lead to ineffective decisions.

Aristotelian causes

The four Aristotelian causes known as material, efficient, formal and final, are summarised in *Physics II 3* and are also found in the dictionary of concepts in the *Metaphysics (V 2)*

> 'Cause' means (1) that from which (as immanent material) a thing comes into being, e.g. the bronze of the statue and the silver of the saucer, and the classes which include these. (2) The form or pattern, i.e. the formula or the essence, and the classes which include this (e.g. ratio 2:1 and number in general are causes of the octave) and the parts of the formula. (3) That from which the change or the freedom from change first begins, e.g. the adviser is a cause of the action, and the father a cause of the child, and in general the maker a cause of the thing made and the change-producing of the changing. (4) The end, i.e. that for the sake of which a thing is, e.g. health is the cause of walking. … all these are for the sake of the end, though they differ from one another in that some are instruments and others are actions. … These then are practically all the senses in which causes are spoken of, and as they are spoken of in several senses it follows that there are several causes of the same thing… (Ross 1955 : 56-57).

It is important to stress this last point; what is referred to as 'causes' is strictly speaking *four senses* in which we speak of cause, and the formal unity of these distinct meanings is established through the question 'why?' (*dia ti*). In *Metaphysics*, Aristotle explicitly says that:

> … causes are spoken of in four senses. In one of these we mean the substance, i.e. the essence (for the 'why' is reducible finally to the formula, and the ultimate 'why' is a cause and principle); in another the matter or substratum, in a third the source of the change, and in a fourth the cause opposed to this, the purpose and the good (for this is the end of all generation and change). (Ross 1955:44-45).

Although Aristotle stresses the interdependence of causes, for some time his approach was interpreted as giving priority to final cause, to teleology. However, as W. Wieland argues in *The Problem of Teleology* (1975: 141-160), the interpretation given to Aristotle's emphasis on teleology, was mistaken. Although an important element in his science, final cause or *telos*, was not the universal and supreme principle of Aristotle's physics. Furthermore, according to Wieland, the concept of *telos* is so conceived that in itself it leaves open the possibility of chance. (ibid:143) This interpretation is closer to our view of a complex non-linear and non-deterministic world. Aristotle saw chance as introducing an 'as if' teleology, which is present if '*a goal is reached, although* there was *no intention* to reach it as such.' (ibid:144).

Another point Wieland makes is that 'no final cause is *just* a final cause' (ibid:145) and that '*telos* is a *concept of reflection* … and not a universal cosmic or metaphysical principle' (ibid:146). So what has been taken for centuries as a doctrine in the sense of a theorem which admits of deductive proof, is 'simply an aid in the quest for particular causal connections' (ibid:147) and may be seen as the classification of the points of view which are adopted in answering the question 'why?'. Wieland concludes the argument by equating the importance of the four causes 'the very fact that the final cause stands on the same level conceptually as the other three causes makes it unlikely that it is the universal principle of nature from which everything can be derived.' In other words the four causes are inter-dependent and final cause or telos does not have primacy of place.

According to Aristotle, as interpreted by Mainzer, 'the task of science is to explain the principles and functions of nature's complexity and change'. (Mainzer 1996: 21) This emphasis was a criticism of those philosophers of nature who identified their principles with individual substances. An individual plant or animal is not merely the sum of its material building blocks; and nature itself was imagined to be a rational organism whose movements were both necessary and purposeful. (ibid: 22). Aristotle distinguished two types of movement, quantitative change (by increase or decrease in magnitude) and qualitative change (by alteration of characteristics or by change of location). Mainzer, like Wieland, also emphasises the 'why' and describes the four aspects of causality as the causes of changes in answer to the question 'why?'

> Why does a plant grow? It grows (1) because its material components make growth possible (*causa materialis*), (2) because its physiological functions determine growth (*causa formalis*), (3) because external circumstances (nutrients in the earth, water, sunlight, etc) impel growth (*causa efficiens*), (4) because, in accordance with its final purpose, it is meant to ripen out into the perfect form (*causa finalis*). (Mainzer 1996: 22).

Another important interpretation of final cause is given by Juarrero (2002) (citing Furley 1978, 1994) as *the object of desire*. She describes how a gazelle becomes a final cause when it is *perceived* by a lion *as food* and hence as an object of desire.

The point made by Juarrero is that 'Awareness (intentionally characterized) and the goal-directedness it supports are the hinges connecting the inside and the outside. … By positing something outside the organism as final cause or object of desire of voluntary behaviour, he (Aristotle) effectively embeds the organism in the environment. An organism's internal state is dependent on something outside it.' This is the sense of final cause that the case study will explore.

By the early seventeenth century, however, Aristotelian final cause was made redundant, as Newtonian mechanics did not allow 'either objects in the external world or anticipated end-states to serve as intentional objects of desire and goals of action'. (Juarrero 2002: 21) When wholes became reducible to the sum of their component parts, and were causally impotent epiphenomena, then the notion of final cause itself became meaningless. However, as will be argued later, the emergent whole may be seen as having a causal relationship with the interacting parts that created the whole and that emergence is both a bottom-up and top-down process. Furthermore, Ilya Prigogine, in his work on dissipative structures showed the irreversibility of time's arrow and by reinterpreting the Second Law of Thermodynamics; he showed that time-irreversible processes are a source of order and that the arrow of time need not be associated with disorder. Dissolution into entropy is not a necessary condition – but *'under certain conditions, entropy itself becomes the progenitor of order.'* (Prigogine & Stengers 1985: xxi).

For 300 years, causal processes were seen as reversible and determinism offered the possibility of predicting exactly the state of the system at any future instant. It was claimed that once the laws of nature and the initial conditions for the universe were fully specified, complete and accurate knowledge of both past and future would be possible. This belief has penetrated so deeply into our consciousness that some scientists still believe that given enough information and computer power the future can be predicted accurately. Complexity science on the other hand has shown that this ambition is unlikely to be achieved, as non-linearity does not usually allow the specific prediction of particular actions or states.

An Argument from Complexity

What distinguishes complex from complicated systems is what Nicolis and Prigogine (1998) called the *creation of new order* and *coherence*. When systems are pushed far-from-equilibrium, by an external constraint or perturbation, at the critical point of bifurcation, the components in a system explore the space of possibilities, self-organise, create order and new structures emerge, whose precise details are not predictable. Nicolis and Prigogine described an experiment with a Bénard Cell and showed that what in classical thermodynamics was considered as waste (heat transfer or dissipation), in the Bénard Cell had created new order. Furthermore, the particles behaved in a coherent, but indeterminate way, despite the random thermal motion of each of them; they described coherence thus: 'everything happens as if each element was watching the behaviour of its neighbours and was taking it into account so as to play its own role adequately and to participate in the overall pattern'. (ibid: 13) Coherence is what distinguishes a system from a random collection of elements, as they form a pattern with specific inter-relationships and inter-dependencies and make up a coherent whole.

But it does not do this in a vacuum – it is influenced by its environment, its history and by the irreversibility of time. 'When a constraint is sufficiently strong, the system can adjust to its environment in several different ways. Stated more formally, *several solutions* are possible for the *same parameter values*. Chance alone will decide which of these solutions will be realized. The fact that only one among many possibilities occurred gives the system a *historical dimension*, some sort of 'memory' of a past event that took place at a critical moment and which will affect its further evolution.' (Nicolis & Prigogine 1998: 14) Furthermore, when later in that chapter they describe the chemical reaction known as the Belousov-Zhabotinski (BZ) reaction they emphasise the importance of the system's past history, as 'the specific path of states followed depends on the system's past history' (ibid: 24). This phenomenon is called *hysteresis*.

Environment, history and context therefore play an important role in the behaviour of complex systems, and cannot be ignored. To understand that behaviour, the notion of context-sensitive and context-independent constraints, needs to be explored, as well as the process of emergence, which may lead to a rethinking of the concept and meaning of causality.

Juarrero (2002, Ch 9) describes context sensitive and context independent constraints as causes. In earlier chapters she showed how according to non-linear, far-from-equilibrium science, systems are created from interacting components, which they then in turn, control. Because of the relationship between parts and wholes, dynamical whole systems are not epiphenomenal, as Newton assumed, but actively exercise causal power over their components. She then attempts to analyse the type of cause at work in dynamic inter-level relationships, both bottom-up and top-down, as the workings of constraint. In particular she shows how intentions can cause behaviour in a top-down process; and this paper builds on her work to show how final cause can be thought of as an emergent process. (ibid: 131)

The notion of constraint was first used in physical mechanics to describe the way the motion of a simple pendulum is 'compelled by the geometry of its environment to move on some specified curve or surface' (Lindsay 1961: 239, in Juarrero 2002) and that particles are connected by rods and strings and cannot, therefore, move any which way. What Lindsay suggests and Juarrero (2002: 132) explains is that constrains may 'compel' or 'force' behaviour, not as a force external to the system, but as the result of the *connection* between elements (in the pendulum) by rods, cords or strings, as well as the *context* or *environment*, in which the object is situated. However, not all environments constrain; for example unrelated aggregates do not constrain their parts, it is only when the components are unified and have become elements in a 'system' or a coherent whole, that parts acquire relational properties as part of a unified systematic whole.

The usual interpretation of the term 'constraint' is that of limiting or closing off of alternatives. However, some constraints not only reduce the number of possibilities, but at the same time create new possibilities. For example, being a member of an organization both restricts certain behaviours, as well as making others possible by virtue of being a member of that organization, which an individual would not have on his/her own. Furthermore, following Aristotle, constraints effect change. (Juarrero 2002:134).

Context-free constraints (Gatlin 1972 in Juarrero 2002), are those that impose some change but do not bring about organization, form or structure ' … if particles are independent of one another, no increase in number will ever produce organization. Heaping more individual and disconnected grains on a sand dune will never turn it into a sand castle.' (Juarrero 2002:136). Although it may cause a landslide and show self-organised criticality.

Components on the other hand become context dependent, in a complex dynamical system, when the behaviour of each molecule suddenly depends both on what the neighbouring molecules are doing and on what happened in the immediate past. Hence the emergence of Bénard Cells and B-Z chemical waves indicate the spontaneous appearance of context-sensitive constraints in far from equilibrium conditions. 'This discontinuous change occurs when previously unrelated molecules suddenly become correlated in a distributed whole.' (Juarrero 2002:139). Furthermore, by making the current states and behaviour of a system dependent on its history, feedback also incorporates the effects of time into those states and behaviour patterns. It is the dependence of the current state partly on previous states, that makes a complex system dynamical and feedback threads a system not only through time and space but relates it closely to its environment. 'Once the system's subsequent behaviour depends on both spatial and temporal conditions under which it was created and the contingent experiences it has undergone, the system is historically and contextually embedded in a way that near-equilibrium systems of traditional thermodynamics are not.' (ibid: 140). Juarrero argues that because time and space are an integral part of dissipative structures, as distinct from their Newtonian equivalent of aggregated atoms, their emergent behaviour is not predictable in detail. History and context therefore partly determine the current and future states, properties and behaviours of complex systems.

When the water molecules in the Bénard Cell self-organise they are not independent of each other, the behaviour of each molecule depends on what the others are doing. Each part therefore is related to the whole, and creates the Bénard Cell as a bottom up process, while at the same time the emergent whole, influences the behaviour of each part. The emergent organism-environment whole, therefore, exerts top-down causality on the parts. What Juarrero calls 'second-order contextual constraints' (ibid:143) thus restrict the degree of freedom of the parts. In this way the system 'preserves and enhances its cohesion and integrity, its organization and identity … Second order contextual constraints are thus in the service of the whole. They are, also therefore, the ongoing, structuring mechanism whereby Aristotle's formal and final causes are implemented.' (Ulanowicz 1997 cited by Juarrero 2002:143). Although the constraints that wholes impose on their parts are restrictive in one sense, at the same time they are creative in that previously independent parts, acquire functional characteristics as part of a whole that were not available to the parts when independent and separate. The newly created emergent system as a whole, also acquires greater potential in that more options are open to it, than to the uncorrelated components. Complex dynamical systems are therefore more than the sum of their parts and therefore different from and irreducible to their aggregation (Juarrero 2002:150).

Some Practical Applications

The following examples, from a global organization, are part of a project within the complexity research programme at the London School of Economics. The approach taken was collaborative action research and was based on semi-structured interviews, in-depth analysis, reflect-back workshops and other workshops and meetings with a variety of stakeholders at all hierarchical levels. The research process included facilitated workshops with the top IT team to identify an inter-related set of social, cultural, technical, physical, economic, political, as well as other conditions. These multiple inter-related conditions or causes (in Aristotelian terms) together created an enabling environment, which facilitated the improvement in alignment between the IT (information technology) department and one of the company's businesses. The findings were analysed using ten principles of complexity theory. (Mitleton-Kelly 2003).

When the global organization, went through a merger a few years ago the IT Director took the opportunity to initiate some changes. His objective was to improve the relationship between the business and the IT department, although he was uncertain how this might be achieved or what it might look like. What emerged was a much closer integration or alignment between IT and the business – a new emergent whole was created that changed the interaction at a macro level between the two parts of the business. At the same time it also affected the way that individuals worked and related. The emergent process had certain emergent outcomes that influenced the interacting individuals and teams. Furthermore changes happened at many and different levels. If causality is seen as part of that emergent process, then it may be thought about in terms of multiple non-linear inter-related influences at different levels, and thus address the first point made in the introduction. An example may illustrate this assertion.

Most IT functions are represented at Board level by the Finance Director. In the post merger company (to be referred to as Tical) the head of IT was invited to become a Director and sit on the Board. He observed how other departments determined their budget and started changing his approach. The traditional approach for heads of IT was to argue for and justify new IT projects and to try to get agreement from the Board. What he decided was that:

> We should have a budget that gets formed through the strategic planning process and any IT investment that needs to be made should be part of the business investments. It's not really for an IT person to justify, it's for the commercial people or whoever to justify as part of their overall investment strategy. Now the budget might be held by me in the IT function to do the IT work, but actually it's being justified as part of some business change programme, and this is all related to the fact there's no such thing as IT projects.

The last phrase is significant. What the Director of IT (DirIT) is saying is that there are no IT projects only business projects that happen to have an IT component. This is not only very unusual it also illustrates a major change in ways of thinking. Thus, three or four years later…

> … it's just accepted that that's the way that things are done. So if any of the commercial people want to undertake a project that requires IT, they talk about how they're going to engage the IT people in understanding what needs to be done from a business point of view so that the IT people will support the IT investment.

In other words both the DirIT and the other Board members influenced each other and changed the way they thought about how IT investments were made, what IT projects meant, who 'owned' them and where the initiatives lay. Their thinking and consequently their behaviour and their relationship *co-evolved* through reciprocal influence. (*Co-evolution* needs to be distinguished from adaptation, which is a one-way process that occurs when the entity *adapts to* changes in its environment. By contrast, co-evolution happens when the interacting entities, *co-evolve with* their broader ecosystem. It is often difficult to observe co-evolution in the short term, and what is apparent may be short-term adaptation of each entity, as part of a longer-term co-evolutionary process.) (Mitleton-Kelly 2003) This co-evolutionary process created a new emergent outcome, a culture that affected the relationships throughout the organization, including the alignment between the IT and the business teams.

The cultural change in Tical shifted the emphasis, following the merger, and was based on greater collaboration and consultation. It was a genuine involvement of everyone in the organization to co-create a new culture, which affected the organisational social ecosystem. Although the improved alignment between the IT professionals and the business managers was part of that whole, it can be seen in itself, as a final cause or intentional object of desire or goal in a particular context. However, the specific outcome was neither determined nor predicted in detail in advance, in the sense that the desire for improved alignment was a relatively nebulous and amorphous desire; the precise way in which it finally manifested itself could have been otherwise. The outcome was therefore emergent. The process itself shaped and guided the final cause, while not fully determining it. This addresses the second point made in the introduction. The third point is that emergence needs to be thought of both as a top-down and a bottom-up reciprocal process, as well as an emergent outcome.

The next example helps to illustrate that the new emergent (and continuously emerging) culture of greater collaboration and consultation, as well as the desired closer IT/business alignment, (a) affected relationships at other levels and (b) was a top-down and a bottom-up process.

A female employee in sales support had a team which supported the sales force. If the sales representatives wanted any items, such as samples, which they offered to their customers, they placed an order on the IT system and her team was then responsible for providing them.

> Now this lady was not satisfied at all with the way that IT did things, and because of this relationship forming exercise, … that sort of view has completely reversed and she now comes down a lot and talks to the person who supports these systems and in fact, she comes and gives them awards for the work that they do for her. So from being a

> very antagonistic person as far as IT was concerned, or having a poor view, she has now changed completely, and these people are now stars that are helping her do whatever it is she does with these rep systems.

Part of the change process was that the IT professionals changed the way they were thinking. They went from focusing on the IT system they were building (i.e. focusing only on the technology) to the output itself. They also changed quite significantly in the way they interacted with others outside the IT team. The environment in the organization as a whole, placed greater emphasis on relationships and this was reflected by the IT team who themselves started to value 'people skills' and the development of relationships. These are unusual characteristics for IT professionals (Mitleton-Kelly 2004b) and this significant change illustrates quite clearly the shift from a technical to a socio-technical approach. In addition the physical environment of co-location made interaction easier. Furthermore, the value contributed by the IT systems was continuously measured in financial terms, and this provided an economic incentive. The point is that there are multiple inter-related causes that together create a social ecosystem. They can be analysed into social, cultural, technical, physical, economic, political, legal and other conditions to help us understand them, but they cannot be pulled apart and isolated as individual causes. Aristotle chose to name them material, efficient, formal and final cause. We might choose to list them as above, but the main point they have in common is that they are intimately related and they co-evolve as Kaminska-Labbe et al (2006) argue so convincingly. Kaminska-Labbe, McKelvey and Thomas also point out that 'If all four Aristotelian causes co-exist in organizations, however, we should find their causal streams intertwining and mutually influencing each other, creating a co-evolution of *causalities* - not only of entities!'

However, as argued above when describing the Board, it is possible to think of relationships *as co-evolving* as well as *causalities* and *entities*. In a complex social system all three co-evolve. It is worth pointing out that, in a human context, the entities that change are usually institutions, not humans themselves as biological entities. The meaning of 'co-evolution', when applied in a human context, needs to be distinguished, from that which is used in biology.

As part of the developing and co-evolving relationship between the sales support team and the IT team they also came to understand the constraints and restrictions imposed by limited resources. Expectations therefore became more realistic, while at the same time the two teams worked together to address those restrictions to mutual benefit.

> … whereas before we had people who would just code things for the system and if they got passed through the chain that we had a required change, they would do the required change and they would do it as it fitted in with whatever stream of work they're being given to do. Now this lady and some of her team talk to the people who are making the changes and they decide between them what is the right thing to do and how it can be done. But also she seems to understand that they can't do everything – that they can only do a limited number of things.

Several things happened in this co-evolutionary process. The IT and sales support teams influenced each other and as a result they changed their way of thinking about each other, they also changed their way of working and the way they related to each other. The latter was fundamental – the more they talked face-to-face, the more they understood and appreciated each other's concerns and challenges, but also each other's needs and requirements as well as the contribution they could each make to support the sales reps. In this case, supporting the sales reps more effectively, may be seen as a final cause. How it was to be done was uncertain – the sales support team leader and the IT team explored alternative ways of working and relating. They *explored their space of possibilities* to overcome the constraint of limited resources and to achieve the objective of supporting the sales representatives. Complex systems are remarkably good at being creative when meeting a constraint as they explore alternative options before they find an appropriate solution, for that particular context (any single solution, is only appropriate within a particular context at a specific time, and will need to change and co-evolve with its changing environment). (Mitleton-Kelly 2003).

Also part of the process was the principle of *self-organization*. The female team leader decided that some changes were necessary in order to improve her support of the sales reps and went to see the IT team. No one directed her or asked her to do so. She and the IT team decided what to do, how to do it, and when to do it. The fact that they were able to do this without external direction or asking for permission was another manifestation of the changed organisational culture. Self-organization is described by Kaminska-Labbe et al (2006), as 'Agents self-organize to create learning, novelty, and new social structures by interacting with, and learning from, each other, coevolving in reaction to each other, revising their behaviour continually'.

Self-organization is essential in the *creation of new order* when pushed *far from equilibrium*. As explained above when discussing the work of Prigogine, and the Bénard Cell, individual elements need to be able to *self-organise* and to *explore their space of possibilities* to find new alternative solutions that are *emergent*. In a human context, far from equilibrium means that an organization is pushed away from its established procedures and ways of working. The merger created the far from equilibrium conditions, which facilitated self-organization and exploration, as new ways of working and relating needed to be found to make the desired new culture work. The process was emergent and was a dual top-down and bottom-up process. It both limited options and at the same time opened up new possibilities.

Another interesting and important aspect in this analysis is that the final cause or desired outcome is not the last element in the causal multi-threaded process. There is no final act. Each emergent outcome, at any macro level, becomes part of the overall process of micro-agent interaction in the complex system and is part of a greater whole. Thus improving the relationship between the IT and business teams is itself part of the broader context of creating a collaborative culture in Tical; while at the same time, being influenced by and influencing the broader culture.

This brings us back to Juarrero's *context dependent constraints*. To reiterate, because of the relationship between parts and wholes, dynamical whole systems actively exercise causal power over their components. Components, or in this case individuals and teams, become context dependent, when the behaviour of each individual/team depends both on what the related individuals/teams are doing and on what happened in the immediate past. Furthermore, by making the current states and behaviour of a system dependent on its history, feedback not only incorporates the effects of time into those states and behaviour patterns, but also relates the systems closely to its environment. The two teams changed both their internal environment, but also the broader environment by improving the work of the sales reps, who in turn were able to work better with their customers. The whole process was enabled by feedback and active communication.

What was traced above, in the two examples at Board level and at the level of two support teams, was a co-evolutionary process with multiple causal elements, operating at several levels and creating emergent outcomes that became part of a larger process of multiple causation. At the same time, the overall process was both top-down from the Board and bottom up from the way individuals and teams interacted and related with each other. They were constrained in that they could no longer continue with previous work patterns, while at the same time new possibilities were opened up for them.

The above were part of other changes in Tical. One example was that as a result of a consultation exercise the 'Directors' corridor' was taken away and all Directors worked close to their teams, not in an isolated block. Furthermore, the IT and Business teams were co-located on the same floor so that they could talk to each other easily and improve their relationships. The IT group had a strong leadership team, but acknowledged that it did not have all the answers and actively sought knowledge and advice from others. They also acknowledged that there wasn't a single solution to the way they worked and were constantly exploring alternative solutions. This exploration however is only possible in a non-blame culture, and this was another emergent outcome.

They also recognised the necessity for a dual top-down, bottom-up approach in leadership. Although they had active leadership and were consistent in terms of talk and action, they also developed a policy of involvement and exploration and were courageous enough to allow ideas to develop, evolve and *emerge*. They therefore created a climate where everyone was willing to interact and this helped to create the right environment for IT to achieve greater alignment with the business.

All this, however, was not done from purely altruistic motives. The closer alignment between IT and the business meant that they derived more value from IT as well as reducing costs. They measured the value IT added to the business in financial terms and in one case alone, they generated over £50m p.a. of new business. At the same time, they recognized that people work best when their contribution is rewarded, not necessarily in terms of money, but as a bottle or champagne or a box of chocolates offered in recognition of that contribution. They even developed what they called the 'fun model' of work.

Conclusion

The above examples show that there were several inter-related causes that together contributed to the new emergent whole. In Aristotelian terms the material, efficient and formal causes were the physical environment of co-location, the taking away of the Directors' corridor, the members of the Board, their motives and interactions, their mind sets, their predisposition to explore alternatives, as well as those of all the other employees and teams throughout Tical, who were prepared to work together following the merger to create something new, rather than imposing one culture on the other. (Mitleton-Kelly 2004a) There were also several final causes. One final cause was the new emergent culture based on collaboration and consultation, co-created by the organization as a whole. Another was the improved alignment between the IT and support teams. Yet another was the improved support of the sales reps who themselves were able to provide a better service to their customers, and so on. All played a part. Hence the four Aristotelian causes and the way that they interact and influence each other are all essential in understanding the causal interactions in organizations (Kaminska-Labbe 2006). They co-evolve and together create emergent new processes and outcomes. Outcomes are neither predictable not repeatable and not necessarily always desirable; they are value-free. (Baskerville & Land, 2004).

The analysis given in this chapter is a mere summary of a rich and complex process, yet it still shows that to understand Tical's enabling environment, it is essential to identify the many inter-related causes. The full analysis will help the organisation understand the underlying principles that facilitated improved alignment; and these principles may be used to guide other parts of the global organisation to create environments that facilitate alignment, in their particular context. Such an approach is far more likely to succeed than one which singles out one or two causes and copies them as 'best practice'. Furthermore, it has helped Tical to make sense of its co-creation process and it helped improve decision-making by providing a full context.

PART 4
Conclusions

Chapter 10

Conclusions – After This Book was Written

Mika Aaltonen

There are many who say that strategic work is all about execution. For *The Third Lens* the way we make sense of our world is the vital activity. Perhaps arguing that sense-making is more important than decision-making, is provocative, but stating that in today's strategic landscapes the most significant decisions involve sense-making rather than decision-making requires some explanation. We may consider that sense-making precedes decision-making because before we make decisions, we have to make sense of a situation, or that sense-making and decision-making are inseparable, as decision-making is inherent in every sense-making activity. Either way, decision-making begins much earlier than we often comprehend. It starts when we make assumptions and definitions about the future, identify current and emergent events and trends, or create causal relationships between certain people and events. However, if we fail to achieve sense-making that gives a broad and comprehensive understanding of a situation, very little can be achieved even if the foresight derived is brilliantly executed.

In *The Third Lens* the importance of two elements, often neglected in strategic management – the nature of the strategic landscape and time – has been emphasized, in a form that makes them the basis for 21st century strategic management.

The Third Lens sees that order is currently preferred in traditional managers' thinking and daily practices. Furthermore, the nature of the strategic landscape is assumed to be order. We believe, however, that it is important to rethink the properties of strategic landscape. Many things do happen in an orderly pattern, but then again many do not. If we accept this idea, then serious consequences should follow for sense-making and decision-making theory and practice. We may talk about the properties of strategic landscapes by depicting them as ordered, complex or chaotic. The properties they convey are different, the dynamics of action in each of them is different, consequently we should be able to distinguish them and apply different tools and methods accordingly – hence the title multi-ontology sense-making.

In our opinion the temporal world is gaining importance over the physical world. Three factors: 1) the increased number of human beings on the planet; 2) the new technologies that allow us new opportunities to control time, 3) and the explosion of the amount and complexity of the interactions between different times, cultures and realities have led to a break from the linear, unidimensional, Newtonian time frame. We believe that socially and technologically constructed, spatially differentiated concepts of time will characterise the interactions of today's world, and enable us to manage them.

Our conclusion is that more contextually constructed approaches with respect to strategic landscapes and time are required; and that when applied they will lead to more appropriate and more effective outcomes in both sense-making and decision-making.

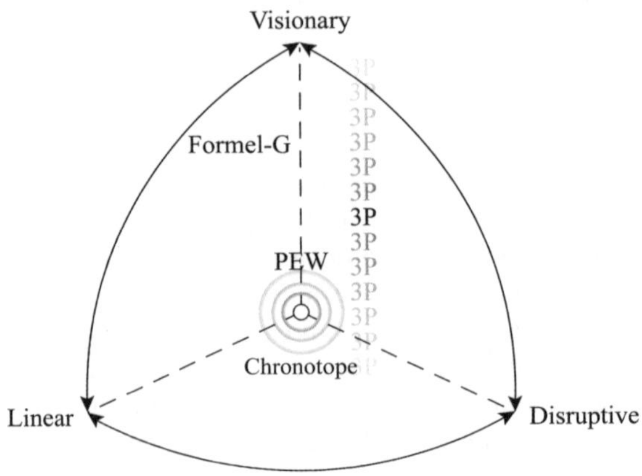

Figure 10.1 Using a chronotope space to reflect upon chapters 4, 5 and 6

The chronotope space is used as a sense-making vehicle for the *Formel*-G, PEW (Political Early Warning) and 3P (Platforms, Pieces and Probabilities) models. They are placed in figure 10.1 to reflect their approximate positions with respect to the strategic landscape and time. By keeping in mind that they all have their respective perspective whether economic, political or general; we can learn from their ways of making sense and responding to their contextually constructed situations.

This kind of sense-making is by nature ex post, the experts and their organizations have already constructed their models, and afterwards we can use the chronotope space to make sense of them. The chronotope space is usually used ex ante, when we face complex sense-making challenges, and need to comprehend trade-offs between different times, cultures and realities, and work out our responses to them.

A chronotope when used by management, employs and possibly combines multiple levels of realities; in essence chronotopes are the causal factors that manage the interconnections between people and events, and shape and increase the effectiveness of strategic decisions, corporate mergers or the timing of press releases, to name just a few examples.

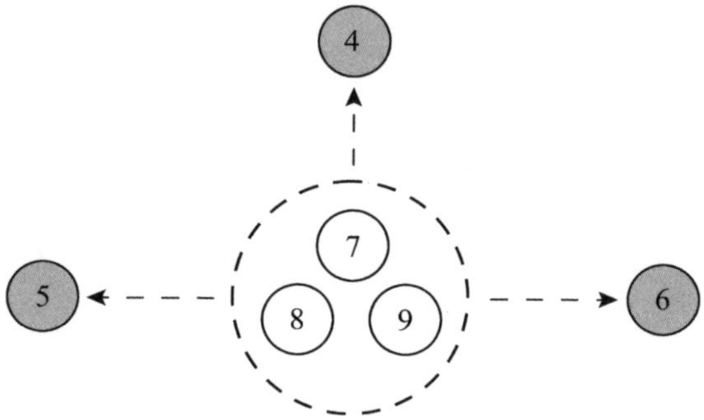

Figure 10.2 Using causal theories to reflect upon chapters 4, 5 and 6

The Third Lens framework, in figure 10.1 has provided the first double-loop that reflects upon each model in chapters 4, 5 and 6 separately and with respect to each other. Figure 10.2 shows how the second double-loop is provided by reframing the cause and effect relationships from three directions: sensitiveness to initial conditions (chapter 7), circular causality (chapter 8) and the re-evaluation of the final cause (chapter 9). Again, only one of them need be used or they can all be used to refresh and challenge models. This would be an ex post kind of second-order learning; as when the models are already in place the alteration of the fundamental beliefs and assumptions upon which they are built are challenged. The reframing of the cause and effect relationships can also form ex ante a fresh basis for the start of modelling, and can be used to guide the modelling of our cognitive frameworks.

Bibliography

Aaltonen, M. (1997), *Suomalaisen johtamisen arvojen ja alkukuvien jäljillä? Myytit ja konnotaatiot lukiolaisten johtamiskäsityksissä*, Publications of the Turku School of Economics and Business Administration. Series A-1:1997.

Aaltonen, M. (2005), 'Methods as Boundary Objects'. *Futura* 2–3/05, 29–38.

Aaltonen, M. and Barth, T. (2005), 'Making Sense of Future. An Analysis of Futures Research Methodology V2.0'. *Journal of Futures Studies*. vol. **9**, Number 4, May 2005, 45-60.

Aaltonen, M. and Barth, T. and Casti, J. L. and Mitleton-Kelly, E. and Sanders, T. I. (2005), *Complexity as a Sensemaking Framework*, FFRC Publications 4/2005.

Aaltonen, M. (2006), 'Circular Cause, Time and Narrativity'. *International Journal of Management Concepts and Philosophy.* v2n3.

Aaltonen, M. and Sanders, T. I. (2006), 'Identifying Systems' New Initial Conditions as Influence Points for the Future'. *Foresight. The journal of futures studies, strategic thinking and policy.* vol. **8**, No. 3, 28–35.

Abele, S. and Bless, H. and Ehrhart, K-M. (2004),'Social information processing in strategic decision-making: Why timing matters?' *Organizational Behavior and Human Decision Processes* **93**, 28-46.

Abelson, R. (1976), 'Script processing in attitude formation and decision making'. In. *Cognition and Social Behavior*. Eds. Carroll, J.S. and Payne, J.W. Erlbaum. Hillsdale.

Adner, R. and Levinthal, D. (2004), What is not a Real Option: Considering Boundaries for the Application of Real Options to Business Strategy. *Academy of Management Review*, 29, 74-85.

Afanasev, A. (1855-64/1973), *Russian Fairy Tales*, Pantheon Books. New York.

'A Grand Strategy to Reinvigorate US Leadership' (2005), Stanley Foundation Policy Dialogue Brief on the 46th Strategy for Peace Conference, Arlie Center, Warrenton, VA,. 20-22 October. p 3.

Albano, G. L. (2001), 'Strategic Certification and Provision of Quality'. *International Economic Review*, vol. **42**, Issue 1, 267–284.

Albrow, M. (1997), *The Global Age: State and Society Beyond Modernity*, Stanford University Press. Stanford.

Alcalá, F. and Ciccone, A. (2003), 'Trade, Extent of Market, and Economic Growth 1960-1996', *Universitat Pompeu Fabra Working Paper* **765**.

Alexandrou, G and Sudarsanam, S. (2001), 'Shareholder Wealth Effects of Corporate Selloffs: Impact of Growth Opportunities, Economic Cycle and Bargaining Power'. *European Financial Management,* vol. **7**, No. 2, 237–258.

Amis, J. and Slack, T. and Henings, C. R. (2004), 'The pace, sequence, and linearity of radical change.' *Academy of Management Journal*, vol. **47**, No. 1, 15-39.

Annan, Kofi A. (2001), 'Prevention of Armed Conflict', *Report of the Secretary-General*, A/55/985, United Nations, New York.

Annan, Kofi A. (2005), 'In Larger Freedom: Towards Development, Security and Human Rights for All', *Report of the Secretary-General*, 21 March 2005, A/59/2005, United Nations, New York.

Annan, Kofi A. (2006), 'Investing in the United Nations: for a Stronger Organization Worldwide', *Report of the Secretary-General*, A/60/2006, 7 March 2006, United Nations, New York.

Ansoff, I. (1975), 'Managing Strategic Surprise by Response to Weak Signals'. *California Management Review*, Winter 1975, vol. **XVIII**, No. 2, 21-33.

Arbnor, I. and Bjerke, B. (1997), *Methodology for Creating Business Knowledge*. Sage. London.

Argyris, C. and Schön, D.A. (1996), *Organizational Learning II: Theory, Method, and Practice*, Addison-Wesley, Reading.

Asuncion-Mund, J. (2005), 'India rising: A medium-term perspective', Deutsche Bank Research, Current Issues.

Axelrod, R. and Cohen, M. D. (2000), *Harnessing Complexity. Organizationl Implications of a Scientific Frontier*. Basic Books. New York.

Axelrod, R.M. (1976), *The Structure of Decision: Cognitive Maps of Political Elites*. Princeton University Press. Princeton.

Bahktin, M. M. (1981), *The Dialogic Imagination*. University of Texas Press. Austin.

Bak, P. and Chen, K. (1991), 'Self–Organized Criticality'. *Scientific American*, January 1991, 26–33.

Balogun, J. and Johnson, G. (2004), 'Organizational restructuring and middle level manager sensemaking'. *Academy of Management Journal*. vol. **47**, No. 4, 523-549.

Barabasi, A-L. (2002), *Linked - The New Science of Networks*. Perseus, Cambridge (MA).

Barr, P. and Huff, A. S. (1997), 'Seeing is not believing: Understanding diversity in the timing of strategic response'. *Journal of Management Studies*, **34**, 337-370.

Barth, F. (1992), 'Towards a Greater Naturalism in Conceptualising Societies'. In: *Conceptualising Society*. Ed. Kupar, A. Routledge. London.

Barth, T. (2005), 'Introducing Disordered Systems – Towards an Agenda for a Meso-level Analysis of Reflective Actors in Complex Dynamics'. In: *Complexity as a Sensemaking Framework*. Ed. Aaltonen, M. FFRC Publications 4/2005.

Bassanini, Andrea and Stefano Scarpetta (2001), 'Does Human Capital Matter for Growth in OECD Countries?', *OECD Economics Working Papers* No. **282**.

Bassanini, Andrea, Stefano Scarpetta and Philip Hemmings (2001), 'Economic Growth: The Role of Policies and Institutions', *OECD Economics Working Papers* No. **283**.

Bauman, Z. (1998), *Postmodernity and Its Discontents*, Polity Press. Cambridge.

Beach, L. R. (1992), 'Epistemic strategies: Causal thinking in expert and non-expert judgment'. In: *Expertise and decision support*. Eds: Wright, G. and Bolger, F, Plenum Press, New York.

Beck, U. (1986), *Risikogesellschaft. Auf dem Weg in Eine Andere Moderne*, Suhrkamp. Frankfurt am Maine.

Beck, U. and Giddens, A. and Scott, L. (1994), *Reflexive Modernization: Politics, Tradition and Aesthetics in the Modern Social Order*, Polity Press. Cambridge.

Beggs, A. W. (1992), The Licensing of Patents under Asymmetric Information. *International Journal of Industrial Organization*, **10**(2), 171–191.

Berger, P. and Berger, B. and Kellner, H. (1974), *The Homeless Mind. Modernization and Consciousness*, Random House. New York.

Bergheim, S. (2005a), Global growth centres 2020: "*Formel*-G' for 34 economies', *Deutsche Bank Research, Current Issues*.

Bergheim, S. (2005b), 'Human capital is the key to growth – Success stories and policies for 2020' *Deutsche Bank Research, Current Issues*.

Bergheim, S. (2006), 'Live long and prosper! Health and longevity as growth drivers', *Deutsche Bank Research, Current Issues.*

Bergland, B. (1994), "Postmodernism and the autobiographical subject: reconstructing the 'other'". In: *Autobiography and Postmodernism*. Eds: Ashley, K. and Gilmore, L. and Peters, G., University of Massachusetts Press, Boston.

Bertuglia, C. S. and Vaio, F. (2003), *Non linearitá, caos, complessitá. Lé dinamiche dei sistemi naturali e sociali*, Bollati Boringhieri. Milano.

Bhagwati. J. (2004), *In Defense of Globalization*, Oxford University Press, New York, p.93.

Bogner, W. C. and Barr, P. S. (2000), 'Making Sense in Hypercompetitive Environments: A Cognitive Explanation for Persistence of High Velocity Competition'. *Organization Science*, vol. **11**, No 2, March-April, 337-370.

Bond, D. and Meier, P. (2005), 'CEWARN: IGAD's Conflict Early Warning and Response Mechanism', in Ramcharan (ed), *Conflict Prevention in Practice; Essays in Honour of Jim Sutterlin*, Martinus Nijhoff Publishers, Leiden/Boston.

Bourdieu, P. (1994), *Raisons pratiques. Sur la théorie de l'action*, Éditions du Seuil. Paris.

Boutros-Ghali, B. (1996), An Agenda for Democratization, Supplement to reports on democratization, *A/51/761*, 20 December, United Nations, New York.

Bowker, C. G. and Star, S. L. (1999), *Sorting Things Out*, MIT Press, Cambridge, MA.

Brown, S. and Eisenhardt, K. (1998), *Competing on the Edge: Strategy as Structured Chaos*. Harvard Business School Press. Boston.

Castells, M. (1996), *Information Age: Economy, Society and Culture. Vol 1: The Rise of the Network Society*, Blackwell Publishers. Malden, MA.

Castells, M. (1997), *Information Age: Economy, Society and Culture. Vol 2: The Power of Identity*, Blackwell Publishers. Malden, MA.

Castells, M. (1998), *Information Age: Economy, Society and Culture. Vol 3: End of Millennium*, Blackwell Publishers. Malden, MA.

Casti, J. L. (1997), *Would-be Worlds. How Simulation Is Changing the Frontiers of Science*. John Wiley and Sons Inc. New York.

Casti, J. L. (2000), *Five More Golden Rules. Knots, Codes, Chaos, and Other Great Theories of 20th– Century Mathematics*. John Wiley and Sons, Inc. New York.

Cecez-Kecmanovic, D. and Dalmaris, P. (2002), 'Knowledge mapping as sensemaking in organizations'. Net Paper. University of Western Australia.

Chen, J. Q. and Lee, S. M. (2003), 'An exploratory cognitive DSS for strategic decision making'. *Decision Support Systems* **36**, 147-160.

Christensen, C. M. (1997), *The Innovator's Dilemma: When New Technologies Cause Great Firms to Fail*, Harvard Business School Press. Boston, MA.

Christensen, C. M. and Anthony, S. D. and Roth, E. A. (2004), *Seeing What's Next. Using the Theories of Innovation to Predict Industry Change,* Harvard Business School Press. Boston.

Cilliers, P. (1998), *Complexity and Postmodernism. Understanding complex systems*. Routledge, London.

Cilliers, P. (2000), 'Knowledge, Complexity and Understanding.' *Emergence*, **2** (4), pp. 7–13.

Cilliers, P. (2001), 'Boundaries, hierarchies and networks in complex systems.' *International Journal of Innovation Management*, **5** (2), pp. 135–147.

Cilliers, P. (2004), 'Complexity, Ethics and Justice'. *Journal for Humanistics (Tijdschrift voor Humanistiek)* **5** (19), pp. 19 – 26.

Cilliers, P. (2005a), 'Complexity, Deconstruction and Relativism'. *Theory Culture and Society*, **22** (5), pp 255–267.

Cilliers, P (2005b), 'Knowledge, limits and boundaries'. *Futures* **37**, 605-613.

Cilliers, P. (2006), 'On The Importance Of A Certain Slowness. Stability, memory and hysteresis in complex systems', Forthcoming in *Emergence: Complexity and Organization*.

Clegg, S. R. (1989), *Frameworks of Power*, Sage. London.

Cohen, J. F. (2001), 'Environmental uncertainty and managerial attitude: Effects on strategic planning, non-strategic decision-making and organizational performance'. *S. Afr. Bus. Management* **32** (3), 17-31.

Coopey, J. and Keegan, O. and Emler, N. (1997), 'Managers innovations as sense making'. *British Journal of Management*. vol. **8**, 301-315.

CSCS: Center for the Study of Complex Systems, University of Michigan. 'What is the Study of Complex Systems?' <www.cscs.umich.edu>.

Cyert, R. M. and March, J. G. (1963), *A Behavioral Theory of the Firm*, Prentice-Hall. Englewood Hill.

Czarniawska, B. (1997), *Narrating the organization: Dramas of institutional identity*, University of Chicago Press, London.

Czarniawska, B. (1999), *Writing Management. Organization Theory as a Literary Genre*, Oxford University Press.

D´Aveni, R. (1994), *Hypercompetition: Managing the Dynamics of Strategic Manouvering*. Free Press. New York.

Daft, R. and Weick, K. E. (1984), 'Toward a model of organizations as interpretation systems'. *Academy of Management Review* **9**, 284-295.

Davis, I. and Stephenson, E. (2006), 'Ten trends to watch in 2006'. *The McKinsey Quaterly.* 18 January 2006.

Davis, L. N. (2001), 'RandD Investments, Information and Strategy'. *Technology Analysis and Strategic Management*, vol. **13**, No. 325–342.

De la Fuente, A. and Doménech, R. (2000), 'Human Capital in Growth Regressions: How much Difference does Data Quality Make?', *OECD Economics Working Papers* **262**.

Dervin, B. and Foreman-Wernet, L. and Layterbach, E. (2002), *Sense-Making Methodology. Reader*, Hampton Press Inc. New Jersey.

Drago, W. A. (1998), 'Structure as a predictor of strategic planning use'. *Journal of Applied Business Research* **14** (1), 125-136.

Drohan, W. (1997), 'Principles of strategic planning'. *Association Management* **49**, 85-87.

Dru, J-M. (1996), *Disruption. Overturning Conventions and Shaking Up the Marketplace*. John Wiley and Sons, Inc. New York.

Dumitriu, P. (2005), 'History and Evolution of the New or Restored Democracies Movement' in Kanninen, Tapio and Sehm Patomaki, Katarina (eds), *Building Democracy from Manila to Doha; The Evolution of the Movement of New or Restored Democracies*, Helsinki Process Publication Series 9/2005.

Dunphy, D. and Stace, D. (1993), 'The strategic management of corporate change'. *Human Relations*, vol. **46**, No. 8, 905-920.

Durlauf, S. N. and Johnson, P. A. and Temple, J. (2005), 'Growth Econometrics', In: Philippe Aghion and Steven Durluaf (2005). *Handbook of economic growth*, Elsevier.

Easterly, W. and Ross, L. (2001), 'It's Not Factor Accumulation: Stylized Facts and Growth Models', *World Bank Economic Review* **15**, pp. 177-219.

Eisenhardt, K. (1989), 'Making fast strategic decisions in high-velocity environments'. *Academy of Management Journal* **32**, 543-576.

Eisenhardt, K. and Zbaracki, M. J. (1992), 'Strategic decision making.' *Strategic Management Journal* **13**, 17-37.

Emmeche, C. (1997), 'Aspects of complexity in life and science', *Philosophica*, **59** (1997, 1), 47–68.

Eoyang, G. E. (2003), *Voices from the Field. An Introduction to Human Systems Dynamics*. Human Systems Dynamics Institute. Circle Pines.

Eoyang, G. E. (2004), The practioner's landscape. *E:CO Special Double Issue*, vol. **6**, Nos 1-2 2004, 55-60.

Ermarth, E.D. (1992), *Sequel to History: Postmodernism and the Crisis of Representational Time*, Princeton University Press, Princeton.

Fiske, S. and Taylor, S. (1991), Social Cognition. McGraw-Hill. New York.

Florida, R. (2002), *The Rise of Creative Class*, Basic Books. New York.

Forbes, D. P. (2005), 'The Effects of Strategic Decision Making on Entrepreneurial Self-Efficacy'. *Entrepreneurship Theory and Practice*, September, 599-626.

Ford, C. M. (2001), 'The futurity of decisions as a facilitator of organizational creativity and change'. *Journal of Organizational Change Management*, vol. **15**, No. 6, 635-646.

Foucault, M. (1977), *Discipline and Punish: The Birth of the Prison*, Penguin. Harmondsworth.

Frankel, Jeffrey A. and David Romer (1999), 'Does Trade Cause Growth?', *American Economic Review* **89**(3), pp. 379-399.

Friedman, T. (2000), *The Lexus and the Olive Tree*. HarperCollins. London.

Frost, A. J. and Prechter, R. R. Jr. and Collins, C. J. (1999), *Elliott Wave Principle: Key to Market Behavior*. John Wiley and Sons Ltd. West Sussex.

Fuglseth, A. M. and Gronhaug, K. (2003), 'Can computerized market models improve strategic decision-making? An exploratory study', *The Journal of Socio-Economics* **32**, 503-520.

Galambos, J. and Abelson, J. and Black, J. (1986), *Knowledge Structures*. Eribaum Associates. Hillsdale.

Gell-Mann, M. (1995), 'What Is Complexity?' *Complexity*, vol. **1**, No. 1.

Giddens, A. (1990), *The Consequences of Modernity*, Polity Press. Cambridge.

Giddens, A. (1991), *Modernity and Self-Identity*. Polity Press. Cambridge.

Gilmore, L. (1994), *Autobiographics: A Feminist Theory of Women's Self-Representation*. Cornell University Press. New York.

Gioia, D.A. and Donnellon, A. and Sims, H.P. (1989), 'Communication and cognition in appraosal : a tale of two paradigms.' *Organization Studies*. vol. **10**, No. 4, 503-530.

Glenn, J.C. and Gordon, T.J. (2003), *Futures Research Methodology – V2.0*. AC/UNU Millennium Project Publication.

Godet, M. (2001), 'Creating Futures. Scenario Planning as a Strategic Management Tool'. *Economica*.

Goldstein, J. (1994), *The Unschackled Organization*. New York. Productivity Press.

Goodhew, G.W. and Cammock, P.A. and Hamilton, R.T. (2005), 'Managers' cognitive maps and intra-organizational performance differences.' *Journal of Managerial Psychology*. vol. **20**, No. 2, 124-136.

Gould, S.J. (1987), *Time's Arrow, Time's Cycle: Myth and Metaphor in the Discovery of Geological Time*. Cambridge. Harvard University Press.

Graham, K. and Felicio, T. (2006), 'Regional Security and Global Governance; A Study of Interaction between Regional Agencies and the UN Security Council with the Proposal for a Regional-Global Security Mechanism', UNU-CRIS (Comparative Regional Integration Studies programme), Institute for European Studies, Vrije Universiteit, VUB Brussels University Press.

Graham, K., Felicio, T and Tavares, R. (2006), 'Capacity Survey (Part I), A Preliminary Analysis of the Organizational Capacities of Regional and Other Intergovernmental Organizations in the Maintenance of International Peace and Security', UNU-CRIS, Bruges, Belgium, 31 March 2006.

Granovetter, M. (1983), *The Strength of Weak Ties: a Network Theory Revisited*, State University of New York. Stony Books.

Greimas, A.J. (1966), *Sémantique structurale. Recherche de méthode.* Librairie Larousse. Paris.

Habermas, J. (1987), *The Philosophical Discourse of Modernity*, The MIT Press. Cambridge.

Hambrick, D. C. (1987), 'Top Management Teams: Key to Strategic Success'. *California Management Review* **30**, 80-108.

Hamerow, T.S. (1987), *Reflections on History and Historians*, Madison, WI. The University of Wisconsin Press.

Harden, J. (2000), 'Language, discourse and the chronotope: applying literary theory to the narratives in health care', *Journal of Advanced Nursing*, **31** (3), 506-512.

Hasan, H. and Goud, E. (2001), 'Support for the sense-making activity of managers'. *Decision Support Systems* ***31***, 71-86.

Hitchcock, David I. (1997), 'Asian Values and the United States', quoted in John Naisbitt 1997, *Megatrends Asia*, Touchstone, p. 54

Hofmann, Jan (2005), 'Customer sharing', *Deutsche Bank Research. E-conomics* **48**.

Holland, J.H. (1998), *Emergence. From chaos to order.* Oxford University Press, Oxford.

Holstius, K. and Malaska, P. (2004), 'Advanced Strategic Thinking. Visionary Management.' *Publications of the Turku School of Economics and Business Administration*. Series Ae-8:2004.

Hopkinson, G. C. (2001), 'Influence in Marketing Channels: A Sense-Making Investigation'. *Psychology and Marketing*, vol. **18**(5): 423-444.

Huber, G. (1991), 'Organizational learning: The contributing processes and the literatures.' *Organizational Science*, **2**, 88-115.

Ifvarsson, C. (2000), 'Sensemaking in small organizations: a conceptual analysis and tentative synthesis'. Net Paper. Unversity of Technology. Luleå.

Ilachinski, A. (2001), *Cellular Automata: A Discrete Universe*, Singapore: World Scientific Publishing Co.

Ilachinski, A. (2004), *Artificial War: Multiagent-Based Simulation of Combat*, Singapore: World Scientific Publishing Co.

Ilachinski, A. (2006), 'Order, Disorder, Chaos and Complexity: A Physicist's/ Analysts's Perspective', Briefing. Center for Naval Analysis: Alexandria. VA.

Introna, L. D. (2003), 'Complexity Theory and Organizational Intervention? Dealing with (in),commensurability'. *In: Complex Systems and Evolutionary Perspectives on Organizations. The Application of Complexity Theory to Organizations*. Ed. Mitleton-Kelly, E. Pergamon. Amsterdam.

Iwata, Edward (2003), 'Blackout Experts Struggle to Shed Light.' *USA Today*, 10/1/03, A1.

Jacucci, G. (2005), *Interaction as Performance – Cases of Configuring Physical Interfaces in Mixed Media*. University of Oulu Press.

Jervis, R. (1976), *Perception and Misperception in International Politics*. Princeton University Press. Princeton, NJ.

Joerges, B: and Czarniawska, B. (1998), 'The question of technology, or how organizations inscribe the world', *Organization Studies*, **19**, 363-386.

Johansson, F. (2005), *The Medici Effect. Breakthrough Insights at the Intersection of Ideas, Concepts and Cultures*, Harvard Business School Press. Boston, MA.

Johnson, G. and Scholes, K. (2002), *Exploring Corporate Strategy*, 6th edition. Prentice Hall. Harlow.

Johnson, S. (2001), *Emergence: The Connected Lives of Ants, Brains, Cities and Software*, New York: Scribner.

Juarrero, A. (1999), *Dynamics in action. Intentional behaviour as a complex system*, MA: MIT Press, Cambridge.

Juarrero, A. (2002), *Dynamics in action. Intentional behaviour as a complex system*, MA: MIT Press, Cambridge. 2nd Edition.

Kaminska-Labbe, R. and McKelvey, B.T.C., (2006), 'On The Coevolution of Causality: A Study of Aristotelian Causes & Other Entangled Influences', Presented at the Academy of Management Meetings, August 14, Atlanta, GA.

Kanninen, T. (1989), 'Frameworks for the Monitoring of Emergent or Ongoing Conflicts: Possibility and Feasibility of an Internationally Standardized Framework', International Studies Association's Convention, London, March 28- 1 April 1989, Panel T-13; Empirical Studies of International Conflict II: Frameworks for Monitoring of Emergent International Conflicts.

Kanninen, T. (1995), *Leadership and Reform: The Secretary-General and the UN Financial Crisis of the late 1980s*, Kluwer Law International, The Hague.

Kanninen, T. (2003), 'Prevention and Reconciliation in a World of Conflicts', in Luiz Carlos Susin, María Pilar Aquino, and Jon Sobrino (eds). *Reconciliation in a World of Conflicts*, Concilium 2003/5 (London: SCM-Canterbury Press, 2003).

Kanninen, T. and Kumar, C. (2005), 'The Evolution of the Doctrine and Practice of Early Warning and Conflict Prevention in the United Nations System', in B.G.

Ramcharan, *Conflict Prevention in Practice; Essays in Honour of Jim Sutterlin*, Martinus Nijhoff Publishers, Leiden/Boston.

Kauffman, S.A. (1971), 'Articulation of parts explanations in biology and the rational search for them. *Boston Studies in the Philosophy of Science*, ed. by R.C. Buck and R.S. Cohen, vol. **8**, pp. 257–272.

Kauffman, S. (1995), *At Home in the Universe. The Search for the Laws of Self-Organization and Complexity*. Oxford University Press. New York.

Kauffman, S. (2000), *Investigations*, Oxford University Press.

Kennedy, P. (1989), *Rise and Fall of Great Powers; Economic Change and Military Conflict from 1500 to 2000*, New York: Random House.

Keskinen, A. and Aaltonen, M. and Mitleton-Kelly, E. (2003), *Organizational Complexity*. Foreword by Stuart Kauffman. FFRC Publications 6/2003.

Ketchen, J. D. and Snow, C. C. and Street, V. L. (2005), 'Improving firm performance by matching strategic decision-making processes to competitive dynamics', *Academy of Management Executive*. vol. **18**, No. 4, 29-43.

Khalil, E.L. and Boulding, K.E. (eds.),(1996), *Evolution, Order and Complexity*, Routledge, London.

Krems, J. F. (1995), 'Cognitive flexibility and complex prolem solving'. In: *Complex problem solving – the European perspective*. Eds: French, P. A. and Funke, J. Hillsdale. Lawrence Erlbaum, 201-218.

Kuosa, T. (2005), 'A Study on Theories of Society´s Macro-Level Transformation. A Macrohistorical Comparison of Pentti Malaska´s Theory of Societal Change to other Theories of Societal Transformation', *Journal of Futures Studies*, 10(1): 15-30.

Kurtz, C.F. and Snowden, D. (2003), 'The new dynamics of strategy: Sense-making in a complex and complicated world', *IBM Systems Journal*, vol. **42**, No 3, 462-483.

Laplace, P-S. (1825/1986), *Essai philosphique sur les probabilités,* Bourgois. Paris.

Latour, B. (1993), *We Have Never Been Modern*, New York. Harvester and Wheatsheaf.

Leonard, N. H. and Beauvais, L. L. and Scholl, R. W. (2005), 'A Multi-Level Model of Group Cognitive Style in Startegic Decision Making'. *Journal of Managerial Issues*, vol. **XVII**, Number 1, Spring 2005, 119-138.

Lerner, G. (1997), *Why History Matters: Life and Thought*. New York. Oxford University Press.

Letiche, H. (2000), 'Phenomenal complexity theory as informed by Bergson', *Journal of Organizational Change Management*, vol. **12**, No. 6, 545–557.

Llewellyn, S. (1993), 'Working in hermeneutics circles in management accounting research: some implications and applications', *Management Accounting Research*, **4**, 231-249.

Loescher, M. S. and Schoeder, C. and Thomas C. W. (2000), *Proteus. Insights from 2020*, The Copernicus Institute Press.

Lönnrot, E. (1835), *Kalevala*.

Lord, R.G. and Maher, K.J. (1991), 'Cognitive theory in industrial and organizational psychology', *Handbook of Industrial and Organizational Psychology* **2**, Consulting Psychologists Press, Palo Alto, 1-62.

Lorenz, E. N. (1963), 'Deterministic Nonperiodic Flow.' *Journal of the Atmospheric Sciences*, March, 130–141.

Lorenz, E. N. (1993), *The Essence of Chaos*. Seattle. University of Washington Press.

Lundberg, C. G. (2000), 'Made sense and remembered sense: Sensemaking through abduction'. *Journal of Economic Psychology* **21**, 691-709.

Luoma, M. (2006), 'A Play of Four Arenas. How Complexity Can Serve Management Development', *Management Learning*, vol. 37, 101–123.

Lyotard, J.F. (1984), *The Postmodern Condition: A Report on Knowledge*. Manchester University Press, Manchester.

Mager, N. H. (1987), *The Kondratieff waves*. Praeger Publishers. New York.

Mainzer, K. (1996), *Thinking in Complexity: The Complex Dynamics of Matter, Mind and Mankind*. Springer, 2nd Edition.

Mankiw, Gregory N., David Romer and David N. Weil (1992), 'A Contribution to the Empirics of Economic Growth', *The Quarterly Journal of Economics*, pp. 407-437.

March, J. G. (1994), 'Bounded rationality, ambiguity, and the engineering of choice'. *Bell Journal of Economics* **9**, (2), 587-608.

Marion, R. (1999), *The Edge of Organizations: Chaos and Complexity Theories of Formal Social Systems*, Sage Publications. Thousand Oaks.

McIntyre, L. (1998), 'Complexity: A Philosopher's Reflections', *Complexity* **3** (6), pp. 26–32.

McKenna, R. J. and Martin-Smith, B. (2005), 'Decision making as a simplification process: new conceptual perspectives', *Management Decision*, vol. **43**, No. 6, 821-836.

Mclroy, M.W. (2000), 'Integrating complexity theory, knowledge management and organizational learning'. *Journal of Knowledge Management*. vol. **4**, No. 3, 195-203.

Meadows, Donella H., Meadows, Dennis L., Randers, Jorgen and Behrens, William W III (1972), *The Limits to Growth*, New York: Universe Books.

Meadows, Donella, Randers, Jorgen and Meadows, Dennis (2004), *Limits to Growth; the 30-Year Update*, Chelsea Green Publishing Company, Vermont.

Metz, S. and Johnson, V D. II (2001), 'Asymmetry and US Military Strategy: Definition, Background, and Strategic Concepts'. Strategic Studies Institute. Special Report.

Mintberg, H. and Raisinghani, D. and Theoret, A. (1976), 'The structure of 'unstructured' decision processes'. *Administrative Science Quaterly*, vol. **21**, 246-275.

Mintzberg, H. and Westley, F. (2001), 'Decision making: it's not what you think'. *MIT Sloan Management Review*. vol. **42**, 89-93.

Mitleton-Kelly, E. (ed.)(2003), *Complex Systems and Evolutionary Perspectives on Organizations. The Application of Complexity Theory to Organizations.* Pergamon. Amsterdam.

Mitleton-Kelly E. (2003), 'Ten Principles of Complexity & Enabling Infrastructures' in Mitleton-Kelly, E. (ed.)(2003), *Complex Systems and Evolutionary Perspectives on Organizations. The Application of Complexity Theory to Organizations.* Pergamon. Amsterdam.

Mitleton-Kelly E, (2004a), 'Co-Evolutionary Integration: A Complexity Perspective on Mergers & Acquisitions' Presented at 20th EGOS Colloquium July 2004 Ljubljana University, Slovenia and published in *Complexity as a Sensemaking Framework*, Ed. Aaltonen M., Finland Futures Research Centre Publications, 4/2005

Mitleton-Kelly E. 2004b 'The Information Systems Professional as a Hermit: Of Plural Rationalities, Information Rejection and Complexity' in *No Great Breakthroughs Have Ever Been Achieved by Taking Things Seriously: A Festschrift for Michael Thompson*; Marco Verweij and Steven Ney (eds), Innovation: The European Journal of Social Science Research, vol. 17, No. 1, December 2004

Mitroff, I. (1998), *Smart Thinking for Crazy Times: The Art of Solving the Right Problems*, Berrett-Koehler. San Fransisco.

Modell, J. (1997), 'From ethnographies to encounters: difference and others'. *Journal of Interdisciplinary History*, **XXVII,** 481-495.

Morgan, G. (1997), *Imaginization: New Mindsets for seeing, organizing, and managing*, San Fransisco. Berrett-Koehler Publishers, Inc.

Mueller, G. C. and Mone, M. A. and Barker III, V. L. (2000), 'Strategic Decision Making and Performance: Decision Processes and Environmental Effects.' *Academy of Management Proceedings*, 2000.

Mwaura, C. and Schmeidl, S. (2002), *Early Warning and Conflict Management in the Horn of Africa*, Red Sea Press, Lawrenceville, New Jersey/Amara, Eritrea.

Naim, M. 2006, 'Our Inequality Anxiety', p. 95, *Foreign Policy*, May/June 2006.

Naisbitt, J. (1982), *Megatrends. Ten New Directions Transforming Our Lives.* Warner Books Inc. New York.

Naisbitt, J. (1994), *Global Paradox. The Bigger the World Economy, the More Powerful Its Smallest Players.* William Morrow and Company, Inc. New York.

Naisbitt, J. (1995), *Global Paradox*, Avon Books, New York, p.47

Naisbitt, J. (1996), *Megatrends Asia. The Eight Asian Megatrends that are Changing the World.* Nicholas Brealey Publishing. London.

Naisbitt, J. and Aburdene, P. (1986), *Re-inventing the Corporation. Transforming Your Job and Your Company for the New Information Society.* Macdonald and Co Ltd. London.

Naisbitt, J. and Aburdene, P. (1990), *Megatrends 2000. Ten New Directions for the 1990's.*

Naisbitt, J. and Aburdene, P. (1992), *Megatrends for Women.* Villard Books. New York.

Naisbitt, J. and Naisbitt, N. and Philips, D. (1999), *High Tech – High Touch. Technology and Our Search for Meaning.* Nicholas Brealey Publishing. London.

Nathan, M. L. (2004), 'How past becomes prologue: a sensemaking interpretation of the hindsight-foresight relationship given the circumstances of crisis.' *Futures* **36**, 181-199.

Neuhaus, Markus (2005), 'Opening economies succeed: More trade boosts growth', *Deutsche Bank Research. Current Issues.*

Nicolis, G. and Prigogine, I. (1989), *Exploring Complexity*, Freeman.

Niitamo, O. E. (1987), 'Social Indicators as an Information System for Evaluation and Control'. *First Finnish-Soviet Sociology Conference*, Helsinki.

Nonaka, I. and Takeuchi, H. (1995), *The Knowledge-Creating Company*, London. Oxford University Press.

Nosek, J.T. (2004), 'Group cognition as a basis for supporting group knowledge creation and sharing', *Journal of Knowledge Management.* vol. **8**, No. 4, 54-64.

Nutt, P. C. (1984), 'Types of organizational decision processes'. *Administrative Science Quaterly* **29** (3), 414-450.

Nutt, P. C. (2000), 'Context, tactics, and the examination of alternatives during strategic decision making', *European Journal of Operational Research*, **124**, 159-186.

Oldroyd, D. (1999), 'Historiography, causality, and positioning: an unsystematic view of accounting history', *The Accounting Historians Journal*, **26**, 83-102.

Oswick, C. and Keenoy, T. and Grant, D. (2002), 'Metaphor and analogical reasoning in organization theory: beyond orthodogy'. *Academy of Management Review*, vol. **27**, No. 2, 294-303.

Oxford English Dictionary, Shorter (2002), 5th Edition. Oxford University Press.

Parker, L. D. (2004), 'Presenting the past: perspectives on time for accounting and management history'. *Accounting, Business and Financial History* **14**:1, March 2004, 1-28.

Parry, J. (2003), 'Making sense of executive sensemaking. A phenomenological case study with methodological criticism.' *Journal of Health Organization and Management.* vol. **17**, No. 4, 240-263.

Patomaki, H. (2005), 'Is democracy possible without global democracy?', in Kanninen, Tapio and Sehm Patomaki, Katarina (eds), *Building Democracy from Manila to Doha; The Evolution of the Movement of New or Restored Democracies*, Helsinki Process Publication Series 9/2005; pp. 195-209. <www.helsinkiprocess.fi/netcomm/ImgLib/24/89/helsinki_process_publication_series_5_2005.pdf>

Perez, J. (2006), 'China's Role Emerges as Major Issue for Southeast Asia'. *The New York Times*, **14** March.

Perrett, R.W. (1999), 'History, time, and knowledge in ancient India', *History and Theory*, **38**, 307-321.

Pesaran, M. Hashem, Yongcheol Shin and Ron P. Smith (1999), 'Pooled Mean Group Estimation of Dynamic Heterogeneous Panels', *Journal of the American Statistical Association* **94**(446), pp. 621-634.

Pettigrew, A. (1992), 'On Studying Managerial Elites.' *Strategic Management Journal* **13**, 163-182.

Porter, D.H. (1981), *The Emergence of Past: A Theory of Historical Explanation,* Chicago. University of Chicago Press.

Preziosi, D. and Farago, C. (2004), *Crasping the World: The Idea of Museum*, Ashgate. Aldershot.

Prigogine, I. and Stengers, I. (1985), *Order Out Of Chaos: Man's New Dialogue with Nature*, Flamingo.

Rifkin, J. (2002), *The Hydrogen Economy. The Creation of the Worldwide Energy Web and the Redistribution of Power on Earth.* Penguin Group. New York.

Robinson, D. (2000), "Paradigms and 'the myth of framework': how science progresses". *Theory and Psychology*. vol. **10**, No. 1, 39-47.

Rosett, C. (2006), 'How Corrupt is the United Nations', Commentary, 1 April. Foundation for the Defense of Democracies.

Ross, W.D. (ed.) (1955), *Aristotle Selections*, Scribner's.

Roth, M.S. (1981), 'Foucault's history of the present'. *History Theory*, **20**, 32-46.

Russo, E. and Schoemaker, P. J. M. (1992), 'Managing overconfidence', *Sloan Management Review* (Winter 1992), 7-17.

Sanders, T. I. (1998), *Strategic Thinking and the New Science. Planning in the Midst of Chaos, Complexity, and Change*, New York. The Free Press.

Sanders, T. I. (2003), 'What is Complexity?' *Catalogue essay for fine arts exhibit entitled, COMPLEXITY.* Washington, DC: Board of Governors of the Federal Reserve Board, 1–2.

Sanders, T. I. and McCabe, J. A. (2003), *The Use of Complexity Science. A Report to the U.S. Department of Education*, <www.complexsys.org/news.htm>

de Saussure, F. (1916), *Cours de linguistique génerale*. Paris.

Schlesinger, Steven C. (2003), *The Act of Creation; The Founding of the United Nations*, Westview Press, Boulder/Oxford.

Schwenk, C. R. (1984), 'Cognitive simplification processes in strategic decision making'. *Strategic Management Journal* **5**, 111-128.

Schwenk, C. R. and Shrader, C. B. (1993), 'Effects of formal strategic planning on financial performance in small firms: A meta-analysis'. *Entrepreneurship Theory and Practice* **17** (3), 53-64.

Scott, A. (1997), 'Introduction: Globalization: Societal Process or Political Rhetoric?' In: *The Limits of Globalization: Cases and Engineering.* Ed. Scott, A. Routledge. New York.

Scwenk, C. R. (1995), 'Strategic decision making'. *Journal of Management* **21**, 177-207.

Senge, P. (1990), *The Fifth Discipline: The Art and Practice of the Learning Organization*, Doubleday/Currency. New York.

Shaw, P. (1997), 'Intervening in the Shadow Systems of Organizations: Consulting from a Complexity Perspective', *Journal of Organizational Change Management* **10** (3): 235-250.

Shell Global Scenarios to 2025.

Snowden, D. (2005), 'Strategy in the context of uncertainty', *Handbook of Business Strategy*, 47-54.

Snowden, D. and Stanbridge, P. (2004), 'The landscape of management: Creating the context for understanding social complexity.' *E:CO*, vol. **6**, Nos. 1-2, 140-148.

Soleberg, P. O. (1967), 'Unprogrammed Decision Making' *Industrial Management Review*, Spring, 19-29.

Soule, B. M. (2002), 'From vision to reality: Strategic agility in complex times'. *AJIC*, April 2002, 107-119.

Stacey, R. (1993), *Strategic Management and Organizational Dynamics*. Pitman. London.

Stacey, R. (1996), *Complexity and Creativity in Organizations*. Berrett-Koehler. San Fransisco.

Stacey, R (2001), *Complex Responsive Processes in Organizations*. Routledge. London.

Stacey, R. D. and Griffin, D. and Shaw, P. (2000), *Complexity Management. Fad or Radical Challenge to Systems Thinking?* Routledge. London and New York.

Sternberg, R. J. (1995), 'Expertise in complex problem solving: A comparison of alternative conceptions'. In: *Complex problem solving – the European perspective*, Eds: French, P. A. and Funke, J. Hillsdale. Lawrence Erlbaum, 295-321.

Stiglitz, Joseph E. (2003), *Globalization and its Discontents*, W W Norton and Company, New York and London.

Streatfield, P. J. (2001), *The Paradox of Control in Organizations*, Routledge. London and New York.

Sun, P.Y.T. and Scott, J. (2005), 'Sustaining second-order change initiation: structured complexity and interface management' *Journal of Management Development*, vol. **24**, No. 10, 879-895.

Surowiecki, J. (2004), *The Wisdom of Crowds. Why the Many Are Smarter than the few and How Collective Wisdom Shapes Business, Economies, Societies, and Nations*. Doubleday. New York.

Talaulicar, T. and Grundei, J. and Werder, A. v. (2005), 'Strategic decision making in start-ups: the effect of top management team organization and processes on speed and comprehensiveness', *Journal of Business Venturing* **20**, 519-541.

Temple, Jonathan (1999), 'The New Growth Evidence', *Journal of Economic Literature* **37**, pp. 112-156.

Tesser, A. (1978), 'Self-generated attitude change'. In: *Advances in experimental social psychology*, Ed. Berkowitz, L., vol. **11**, 289-338. Academic Press. New York.

Thomas, L. G. (1996), 'The two faces of competition: Dynamic resourcefulness and the hypercompetitive shift', *Organizational Science*, 7, 221-242.

Toffler, A. (1981), *The Third Wave.* Collins. London.

Turcotte, D. L. and Rundle J. B. (2002), 'Self-organized Complexity in Physical, Biological and Social Systems.' *Proceedings of the National Academy of Sciences of the United States of America,* vol. **99**, suppl.1 Washington, DC: National Academies Press, pp. 2463–2465.

Turkle, S. (1997),'Growing up in the culture of simulation'. In: Beyond calculation – the next fifty years of computing. Eds: Denning, P. J. and Metcalfe, R. M. New York. Springer, 93-104.

United Nations (2004), 'High-level Panel on Threats, Challenges and Change 2004, A more secure world: Our shared responsibility', *The report of the High-level Panel on Threats, Challenges and Change*, United Nations, 2004.

United Nations' General Assembly (2005a), Fifty-ninth session Agenda item 53 Question of equitable representation on and increase in the membership of the Security Council and related matters. A/59/L., 64 July 2005.

United Nations' General Assembly (2005b), Resolution adopted by the General Assembly, 2005 World Summit Outcome. A/RES/60/1, 24 October 2005.

United Nations' Secretariat (2005), Assessment of Member States' advances to the Working Capital Fund for the biennium 2006-2007 and contributions to the United Nations regular budget for 2006. ST/ADM/SER.B/668. 27 December 2005.

Van de Ven, A. H. (1980), *Measuring and Assessing Organizations*, Wiley. New York.

Venkatraman, N. (2000), 'Five steps to a dot-com strategy: how to find your footing on the web' *Sloan Management Review* **41** (3), 15-28.

Voss, Silja (2006), 'Mexico 2020: Tequila sunrise', *Deutsche Bank Research. Current Issues*.

Waldrop, M. M. (1992), *Complexity. The Emerging Science at the Edge of Order and Chaos*, Touchstone. New York.

Wallerstein, I. (1974), *The Modern World-System 1: Capitalist Agriculture and the Origins of the European World-Economy in the Sixteenth Century,* Academic press. New York.

Wallerstein, I. (1983), *Historical Capitalism*. Verso Editions.

Walsh, J.P. (1995), 'Managerial and organizational cognition: notes from a trip down memory lane', *Organization Science*. vol. **6**, No. 3, 280-321.

Walters, B. A. and Jiang, J. J. and Klein, G. (2003), 'Strategic information and strategic decision making: the ES/CEO interface in smaller manufacturing companies.' *Information and Management* **40**, 487-495.

Watson, T. J. and Chiappini, F. B. (1998), 'Managerial sensemaking and occupational identities in Britain and Italy: The role of management magazines in the process of discursive construction', *Journal of Management Studies*, **35**, 285-302.

Weick, K. E. (1982), 'Management of organizational change among loosely coupled elements.' In: *Change in Organizations*. Jossey-Bass. Thousand Oaks.

Weick, K. E. (1995), *Sensemaking in Organizations*, Sage. Thousand Oaks.

Weick, K. E. (2001), *Making Sense of the Organization*, Blackwell. Oxford.

Wheatley, M. J. (1999), *Leadership and the new science: discovering order in a chaotic world*, Berrett-Koehler. San Fransisco.

Wieland, W. (1975), 'The Problem of Teleology' in *Articles on Aristotle, 1. Science*, J. Barnes, M. Scholfield, R. Sorabji, (eds.). Duckworth.

Wilson, I. (2003), *The subtle art of strategy*, Praeger Publishers. Westport.

Witte, E. (1972), 'Field research on complex decision making process – The phase theory.' *International Studies of Management and Organization* **56**, 156-182.

Woodside, A. G. (2001), 'Editorial: Sense Making in Marketing Organizations and Consumer Psychology: Theory and Practice', *Psychology and Marketing*, vol. **18** (5): 415-421.

Yakovets, Yu. V. (1999), *Russian Cyclism: Anticipating the 21st Century.* Edwin Meller Pr.

Zimmerman, B. J. and Lindberg, C. and Plsek, P. (1998), *Edgeware: Insights from Complexity Science for Health Care Leaders,* VHA Inc. Inving.

Index

Note: Bold page numbers indicate diagrams & tables; numbers in brackets preceded by *n* are footnote numbers.